Antonia Pérez Arias

Haptic Guidance for Extended Range Telepresence

Karlsruhe Series on Intelligent Sensor-Actuator-Systems

Volume 12

ISAS | Karlsruhe Institute of Technology
Intelligent Sensor-Actuator-Systems Laboratory

Edited by Prof. Dr.-Ing. Uwe D. Hanebeck

Haptic Guidance for Extended Range Telepresence

by
Antonia Pérez Arias

Dissertation, Karlsruher Institut für Technologie (KIT)
Fakultät für Informatik
Tag der mündlichen Prüfung: 13. November 2012

Impressum

Karlsruher Institut für Technologie (KIT)
KIT Scientific Publishing
Straße am Forum 2
D-76131 Karlsruhe
www.ksp.kit.edu

KIT – Universität des Landes Baden-Württemberg und
nationales Forschungszentrum in der Helmholtz-Gemeinschaft

KIT Scientific Publishing 2013
Print on Demand

ISSN 1867-3813
ISBN 978-3-7315-0035-3

Haptic Guidance for
Extended Range Telepresence

zur Erlangung des akademischen Grades eines

Doktors der Ingenieurwissenschaften

von der Fakultät für Informatik
des Karlsruher Instituts für Technologie (KIT)

genehmigte

Dissertation

von

Antonia Pérez Arias

aus A Rúa

Tag der mündlichen Prüfung: 13.11.2012

Erster Gutachter: Prof. Dr.-Ing. Uwe D. Hanebeck

Zweiter Gutachter: Prof. Dr.-Ing./Univ. Tokio Martin Buss

Acknowledgement

The work on this thesis was performed during my time as a research assistant at the Intelligent Sensor-Actuator-Systems Laboratory (ISAS) of the Karlsruhe Institute of Technology (KIT). Working there was a very challenging and also rewarding experience. I would like to take the opportunity to thank all the people who supported me during this time and helped me to successfully conclude this work. First of all, I would like to thank my advisor Prof. Dr.-Ing. Uwe D. Hanebeck for his encouragements, valuable discussions, and support throughout my work at the laboratory. I am also very grateful to Prof. Dr.-Ing./Univ. Tokio Martin Buss for co-supervising this thesis.

I am grateful to all the colleagues at the ISAS for the cooperative and enjoyable atmosphere. Special thanks go to Frederik Beutler for his great advice and tireless help during the first years of my research activities. I must also thank Henning Eberhardt for many fruitful discussions and long evenings of experiments, without which the development of the Plenhaptic Guidance Function would not have been possible.

The development and maintenance of the numerous hardware components of the telepresence system would not have been possible without the active support of the people in the mechanical and electronic workshop. Special thanks go to Hannes Merkle and Wolfgang Rihm for their engagement and valuable contributions in the development of the mechanical and electronic components of the new haptic device.

I would also like to thank all students who contributed to this thesis. Particularly I would like to thank Oliver Richter for his work in the admittance control of the haptic interface, Sebastian Bumm for his contribution in the design of the new haptic device, and Florian Pfaff for his work in the implementation of the haptic guidance and his engagement in all experiments and demos within the telepresence system. Thanks go also to my working students Christian Tesch and Frederik Doll for their productive assistance in many hardware and software issues of the haptic interface, and to all students of the practical lab course who contributed to this thesis.

Finally, I would like to thank above all my family and my boyfriend Jesús Muñoz Morcillo, who always stood behind my decisions and supported me particularly in critical phases. Without all their constant support this thesis would not have come into existence.

Karlsruhe, April 2013   *Antonia Pérez Arias*

Contents

Notation

Conventions

Scalars, Vectors, and Matrices

x	scalar value
$\underline{x}$	vector
$\mathbf{X}$	matrix

Subscripts

$(.)_U$	relative to user or user environment
$(.)_T$	relative to target or target environment
$(.)_O$	in world coordinate frame
$(.)_H$	in local coordinate frame attached to user (usually w.r.t. user's head)
$(.)_G$	goal position
$(.)_E$	end-effector of haptic interface or user's hand position
$(.)_L$	linear prepositioning unit
$(.)_S$	haptic SCARA-manipulator
$(.)_{ref}$	reference value
$(.)_{meas}$	measured value

Symbols

General

S	orthogonal coordinate frame
$^A\mathbf{T}_B$	homogeneous transformation from coordinate frame S_A to S_B

Motion Compression

$\tilde{S}$	curvilinear coordinate system
$\underline{x}$	pose of user as projection on an xy-plane
x, y, ϕ	components of $\underline{x}$
s	path variable
$\kappa(s)$	curvature along the path
$\psi(s)$	orientation along the path
$\underline{c}(s)$	position along the path
$c_x(s), c_y(s)$	components of $\underline{c}(s)$
$\underline{p}$	planning reference point
ψ	start orientation at planning reference point
n	normal deviation from the path
$\Delta\kappa$	curvature difference between the user and the target path

Haptic Information

$\underline{x}$	Cartesian position vector
$\underline{F}$	Cartesian force vector
$\underline{\gamma}$	joint configuration of haptic manipulator
$\underline{\tau}$	torque vector of haptic manipulator
$\underline{d}$	guidance direction
$\mathbf{J}$	Jacobian matrix
$\mathbf{M_m}$	mass matrix of the displayed virtual object
$\mathbf{D_m}$	viscous damping matrix of the displayed virtual object
$\mathbf{M_m}$	stiffness matrix of the displayed virtual object

Glossary

ANOVA	Analysis of Variance
DOF	Degree of Freedom
ERT	Extended Range Telepresence
HM	Haptic Manipulator
HMD	Head-mounted Display
HSI	Human System Interface
JND	Just Noticeable Difference
MC	Motion Compression
PHGF	Plenhaptic Guidance Function
PPU	Prepositioning Unit
SMHI	Semi-mobile Haptic Interface

Zusammenfassung

In der vorliegenden Arbeit werden Verfahren für die haptische Führung eines Benutzers in der weiträumigen Telepräsenz vorgestellt. Bei der weiträumigen Telepräsenz hat der Benutzer den Eindruck, sich gehend in einer entfernten realen oder virtuellen Zielumgebung fortzubewegen. Seine Bewegungen werden einerseits auf den Teleoperator bzw. auf den Avatar in der Zielumgebung übertragen. Andererseits erhält der Benutzer multimodales, visuelles, akustisches und haptisches Feedback aus der Zielumgebung, das ihn die Interaktion mit dieser ermöglicht. Dabei liegt der Fokus auf der haptischen Information, welche dem Benutzer mittels einer haptischen Schnittstelle weitergeleitet wird. Diese Art von Telepräsenz erfordert eine besondere Art haptischer Schnittstellen, welche Krafteindrücke aus der Zielumgebung in der gesamten Benutzerumgebung bereitstellen. Dafür wird in dieser Arbeit eine semi-mobile haptische Schnittstelle verwendet. Zudem wird ein neues Design für den haptischen Manipulator der semi-mobilen haptischen Schnittstelle vorgestellt, das die Bewegungsfreiheit des Benutzers verbessert.

Die haptische Information aus der Zielumgebung, die dem Benutzer einen realitätsnahen Eindruck vermittelt, wird in dieser Arbeit mit einer haptischen Führung augmentiert, um den Benutzer zu bestimmten Zielen in der Zielumgebung führen zu können. Diese haptische Führung sorgt einerseits dafür, dass der Proxy von Hindernissen ferngehalten wird, andererseits kompensiert sie auch unerwünschte durch die Körperdynamik des Benutzers verursachte Bewegungen. Die haptische Information muss dabei so transformiert werden, dass der Benutzer den Eindruck hat, er befinde sich in einer beliebig großen Zielumgebung und wird dort geführt. Dafür werden sowohl die Interaktionskräfte als auch die Führungskräfte zwischen Ziel- und Benutzerumgebung mittels Bewegungskompression transformiert.

Um eine intuitive Führung zu erreichen, die den Benutzer dazu befähigt, eine bestimmte Aufgabe telepräsent durchzuführen, ohne seine Bewegung zu sehr einzuschränken, wird eine passive Führung verwendet. Bei der passiven Führung wird diejenige Bewegung eingeschränkt, die nicht zum Ziel führt. Zudem wird eine kontextbasierte haptische Führung vorgestellt, in der die Führungsintensität abhängig ist von der Geometrie der Zielumgebung und mit der der Benutzer gleichzeitig auf mehrere Ziele geführt werden kann.

Die haptische Information wird an die semi-mobile haptische Schnittstelle gesendet. Diese besteht aus einer langsamen Vorpositionierungseinheit und aus einem schnellen mobilen Manipulator. Für die Darstellung der haptischen Information wird eine Admittanzregelung verwendet, welche einerseits die eigene Dynamik der Schnittstelle kompensiert und andererseits die erwünsche Führung in jeder Richtung darstellt. Da der Benutzer sich in der Zielumgebung frei bewegen kann, muss gewährleistet sein, dass der Benutzer den Arbeitsraum der Schnittstelle nicht verlässt. Die optimale Vorpositionierung der haptischen Schnittstelle sorgt einerseits dafür, dass der haptische Manipulator nah an seiner optimalen Manipulierbarkeit bedient wird, und andererseits, dass dem Benutzer immer die maximale Bewegungsfreiheit zur Verfügung gestellt wird.

Die entwickelten Methoden wurden in einem prototypischen Telepräsenzsystem evaluiert. Die Steigerung der Genauigkeit bei der Verfolgung eines Pfades in einer großen Zielumgebung wurde experimentell bewiesen. Aus den Erkenntnissen der Evaluierung wurden die Anforderungen für das neue Design des Manipulators der semi-mobilen haptischen Schnittstelle hergeleitet. Demnach sollte der neue Manipulator ein deutlich geringeres Gewicht und reduzierte Trägheit aufweisen. Das neue Design erlaubt eine bessere Raumausnutzung in der Benutzerumgebung und fördert darüber hinaus eine erhöhte Benutzersicherheit.

Abstract

This research develops a novel navigation assistance system for *extended range telepresence*, one that aims at intuitively supporting the user without the need for explicit control on his/her part. In extended range telepresence, the user can move around in a distant target environment, either real or virtual. To achieve this, his/her movements in the user environment are transmitted to the proxy, which is either a teleoperator or an avatar, in the target environment. In return, the user receives multimodal, visual, acoustic, and haptic feedback from the target environment.

Haptic feedback provides the user with more complete information and increases the sense of being present in the target environment, thereby improving the user's ability to perform complex tasks. In this work, the haptic information from the target environment is augmented with haptic guidance information in order to assist the user in reaching desired goals while still keeping the user fully in charge of the operation strategy. The haptic assistance also ensures that the proxy is kept off obstacles, and that undesired movements of the user caused by his/her own dynamics are compensated for.

In order to guide the user in arbitrarily large target environments through haptic cues that are applied to the user's hand in the spatially limited user environment, the desired path in the target environment is first transformed with *Motion Compression* into a path that fits into the user environment, and then the haptic information is transformed back into the user environment by using the same mapping linearized at the current user position.

The proposed haptic guidance function, called the *Plenhaptic Guidance Function*, systematically integrates the context information from the target environment and the task in order to easily adapt the guidance to changed conditions and new target scenarios without great effort. In order to achieve an intuitive guidance, two force control methods have been proposed to render the Plenhaptic Guidance Function. With the *active force control method*, the user is guided towards the desired direction by means of an external guidance force. With the *passive force control method*, only user movement that does not lead towards the goal is restricted.

The haptic information is transmitted to the user through a haptic interface. Extended range telepresence requires a special kind of haptic interfaces that display both contact information from the target environment and haptic guidance commands in the entire user environment. The concept of *semi-mobile haptic interfaces*, which consist of a prepositioning unit and a haptic manipulator, is therefore especially suitable for haptic extended range telepresence. In this work, a new semi-mobile haptic interface has been developed, one whose lightweight design and novel setup configuration atop the user provide for an absolutely safe operation of the interface and an optimal utilization of the available space in the user environment, in addition to yielding a high force display quality.

The new configuration considerably simplifies the prepositioning algorithm to decouple the motion of the prepositioning unit and the haptic manipulator. For the transparent display of the haptic information, a direction-dependent admittance control is used, which on the one hand compensates for the interface's own dynamics, and on the other hand furnishes the user with the desired guidance in each direction.

The new semi-mobile haptic interface with *mirror setup configuration* was extensively evaluated to determine its specifications with regard to dexterous workspace, output capability, and backdrivability. Furthermore, an experimental evaluation of the whole system has been carried out in order to investigate the benefits of haptic navigation assistance in a very large telepresent scenario.

1. Introduction

Telepresence is defined by Sheridan in 1989 [112] as the extension of a person's sensing and manipulation capability to a remote location. The concept of telepresence (as well as the concept of *robot*) has its origin in science-fiction literature. While the first autonomous robot appears first in Karel Čapek's play *R.U.R. (Rossum's Universal Robots)* in 1920, the first integrated telepresence system was built by Robert Heinlein's fictional character Waldo in the eponymous novel written in 1942. In this novel, *telemanipulators* (called "waldoes") allow the disabled genius Waldo to perform teleoperations on Earth from a zero-gravity home in orbit around Earth.

It is no coincidence that the first industrial robot was a telemanipulator, developed by R. C. Goertz from the Argonne National Laboratory in order to transport radioactive waste without risk to the human operator. Since then, advances in robotics research have provided robots with increasing autonomy so that robots can relieve humans from many heavy, repetitive, or dangerous tasks. However, there are still many tasks that are subject to unstructured information or unknown factors, tasks that require the cognitive abilities of humans (i.e., their ability to decide and to react to unforeseen events).

Therefore, the motivation behind the development of telepresence systems is to combine the superiority of robots with respect to their physical robustness against environmental conditions, force, endurance, and precision, and the intellectual superiority of humans. A telepresence system is then necessary when the task cannot be automatized and the direct handling of the task by a human is impracticable, too dangerous, or too expensive.

1

A telepresence system consists of three major components: the *human system interface*, the *proxy*, and the *communication channel*. The *human system interface* is the device carried by the human operator, or *user*. The user interacts with the human system interface in the *user environment* and through it indirectly interacts with the remote real or virtual *target environment*. Visual feedback from the remote environment is usually presented through a *head-mounted display* (HMD); acoustic feedback is replayed by headphones; and haptic interactions are enabled by using a *haptic interface*. The *proxy* represents the human operator in the target environment. In a real target environment, the proxy is a *teleoperator*, which interacts with the environment. In the case of a virtual target environment, the proxy is an *avatar*. In this case, the environment and the avatar are models from which the virtual sensory information is synthesized. Between the human system interface and the proxy there is a *communication channel*, e.g., the Internet, for the exchange of sensory and actuatory information. Ideally, the human operator should not perceive any difference between direct interaction with the target environment and interaction via a telepresence system. In this ideal case, the system is called *transparent* and the corresponding measure is *transparency* [73].

The large number of applications of telepresence systems in real target environments include exploration and reconnaissance of remote areas, space maintenance missions, nuclear waste handling, demining of contaminated areas, systems for disaster recovery, tele-surgery, etc. Systems for virtual reality applications also aim to give the user a realistic impression of the virtual target environment, for the following uses, for example: training for evacuations; ergonomic design tests; virtual sightseeing; virtual treatment of phobias; multi-modal games; etc.

1.1. Haptic Extended Range Telepresence

In contrast to static telepresence systems, extended range telepresence systems permit the user to move in an extensive target environment. However, most existing systems assume a static user, who uses devices like joysticks, pedals, or steering wheels to control the position of the proxy. The drawback of these systems is that the user does not receive *proprioceptive* feedback. However, the sense of *proprioception*, the sense of one's motion, is especially important for human navigation and path finding [29, 30]. Such telepresence systems are not intuitive, since they do not exploit all the natural sensory, cognitive, and motor skills of humans.

In the following, the term *extended range telepresence* is restricted to systems, in which the human can use all the aforementioned skills for locomotion in the target environment. In such an *extended range telepresence system*, the user's motion is tracked by a large-scale tracking system, and transferred to the proxy in the target environment. As a result, in extended range telepresence the human operator can additionally use the sense of proprioception to navigate the proxy by natural walking. Such a system is illustrated in Fig. 1.1.

However, without further processing of the motion information, the motion of the operator is restricted to the size of the user environment, which is limited, for example, by the range of the tracking system or the available space. Two kinds of solutions to this problem exist, which can be classified in terms of *mechanical locomotion interfaces* and *algorithmic interfaces*. Mechanical locomotion interfaces hold the user to the spot by sliding the ground under the user's feet. They include passive devices like the commercially available *VirtuSphere* [1] (a large sphere inside which the user walks), omnidirectional treadmills [52, 56, 58], or actively driven floor surfaces [57, 128]. Most locomotion interfaces require not only bulky and mechanically complex setups, but also complex control algorithms. For

---

1   http://www.virtusphere.com

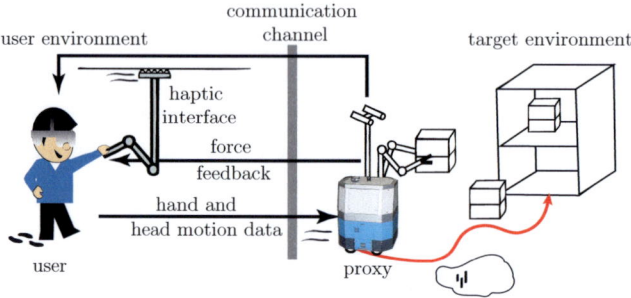

Fig. 1.1.: Extended range telepresence system with haptic interaction.

this reason, in this work, the algorithmic interface provided by *Motion Compression* [83] is used to allow exploration of arbitrarily large target environments. The algorithm Motion Compression solves the problem by mapping the desired path in the target environment to a feasible path in the user environment along which the user actually walks, while minimizing proprioceptive and visual inconsistencies.

Haptic feedback in extended range telepresence systems is the focus of interest in this thesis. Haptic feedback provides the operator with more complete information and increases the sense of being present in the remote environment, thereby improving the ability to perform complex tasks [113]. While the visual and auditory modalities make use of rather advanced techniques that are common to static telepresence systems, the haptic modality in extended range telepresence needs further attention.

1.2. Haptic Navigation Assistance

The technical limitations of real telepresence systems mean that ideal *transparency* cannot be achieved in practice. This is mainly due to restrictions of available hardware components or the implemented control architectures, which are not able to realize a truly transparent interaction with the remote environment. As a result, telepresence's potential to easily transport the abilities of a human to a remote site cannot be fulfilled and the operations performed by means of a telepresence system are typically characterized by an increase in the execution time, failure rate, and stress level of the human operator.

Although navigation in the target environment is more intuitive with extended range telepresence systems than with static telepresence systems, the above mentioned technical limitations such as restricted field of view, time-delays, and in particular inconsistencies caused by the algorithmic interface that makes extended range telepresence possible, complicate the navigation task. To reduce these effects, an assistive system is required to support the human operator in performing the navigation task while still keeping the user fully in charge of the operation strategy. To obtain this objective, a haptic navigation assistive system is proposed in this thesis, a system that aims at intuitively supporting the human operator without the need for explicit control on his or her part.

The purposes of this haptic navigation assistive system are: to help the user find his/her destination in the target environment by reducing task workload; to keep the proxy off certain obstacles or dangerous areas in the target environment; to improve the human performance in complex navigation tasks that require better-than-human accuracy and/or velocity; and to improve skill acquisition for training applications. In addition, the haptic assistance in extended range telepresence serves to guide the user not only in the target environment, but also in the user environment, in order to keep the user inside the limits of the user environment.

1.3. Problem Formulation and Challenges

In the extended range telepresence system with haptic navigation assistance, the haptic feedback signals presented to the user are augmented with haptic guidance information. In order to calculate the guidance commands, the positions of the user and the proxy are assumed to be known in the user environment and in the target environment respectively. Furthermore, knowledge of the positions of possible targets and obstacles is assumed to be gained, for example, by means of additional sensors mounted on the teleoperator and/or a model of the target environment.

A specific challenge of haptic guidance in extended range telepresence is that the user has to be guided in arbitrary target environments, whereas the haptic cues are applied to the user in the spatially limited user environment. Furthermore, if the position of the user and the proxy are related by the transformation provided by Motion Compression [83], the haptic assistance has to guarantee consistent visual and haptic guidance information.

In order to support the user in performing the navigation task without disturbing his/her plans, the haptic guidance system has to be updated based on the intentions of the operator. Moreover, it has to infer how the human would perform the task, and then detect and correct unwanted deviations.

Adequate haptic commands have to be found in order to control the motion of the user by means of forces applied to his/her hand, which means controlling an underactuated system. In addition, since the user has to preserve the control over the task, as well as the feeling of presence in the target environment, a trade-off between controlling the user's motion (which aims at improving task performance) and leaving the user enough freedom (in order to be in charge of the task) has to be achieved.

Finally, an adequate haptic interface is required in order to provide the user with haptic guidance information in extended range telepresence systems. On the one hand, this haptic interface must be able to display forces in the whole user environment, and on the other hand, the forces must be displayed while the user is walking. Although there are many commercially available interfaces, most existing haptic interfaces have only a small workspace and a low output capability. The design and the control of a haptic interface for extended range telepresence should guarantee not only an unrestricted workspace, but also a transparent display of haptic information from the target environment, high maneuverability, and high user safety.

1.4. Main Contributions and Outline of the Dissertation

1.4.1. Main Contributions

The goal of this thesis is the development of a novel haptic navigation assistance system for extended range telepresence. The three major contributions of this thesis are listed below.

- A novel framework that provides haptic assistance in arbitrarily large target environments is presented. This framework combines the wide-area guidance concept with Motion Compression. To achieve consistent haptic and visual guidance, the current intended path is transformed with Motion Compression into a path that fits into the user environment. The same nonlinear mapping between the user and the target environment, linearized at the current user position, is then used to transform the haptic guidance commands back into the user environment.

- In the proposed assistive telepresence system the user can change both the goal and the desired path on the fly. This is possible because the calculation of the guidance information, which is represented by the *Plenhaptic Guidance Function* (PHGF), relies on a human locomotion model, the *goal-directed* locomotion model. With *goal-directed guidance*, the calculation of the optimal target path (which leads to the current intended goal and that helps the user avoid the obstacles), as well as the transformation of the intended path into the user environment are performed dynamically at each time step.

- A kinematic and dynamic model of the user as an underactuated system was applied to render the guidance information of the PHGF as *active* and/or *passive* haptic cues, which applied on the user's hand control the motion of the user along the desired direction. The optimal strength of the haptic guidance has been found experimentally based on static relationships between task performance and human effort.

- A new Semi-mobile Haptic Interface (SMHI) has been developed, which makes it possible to provide the user with haptic guidance information as well as contact information without workspace restrictions while simultaneously increasing the maneuverability of the device and achieving a safer operation. The concept of semi-mobile haptic interfaces consisting of a prepositioning unit and a haptic manipulator has been improved by placing the haptic manipulator on top of the user. In this new design, called *mirror configuration*, the haptic manipulator is designed and controlled in such a way that it reflects the planar workspace of the human's arm. This novel configuration has the further benefit that fast motions of the human's hand are undertaken by the haptic manipulator, while undesired inertial forces caused by fast motions of the prepositioning unit are avoided.

1.4.2. Outline of the Dissertation

In Chapter 2, a classification of existing assistance paradigms and haptic interfaces is presented. Most existing literature about haptic assistance is basically concerned with telepresent or cooperative manipulation systems, which assume a static user. The same occurs with most existing haptic interfaces. Although there are essentially two types of haptic interfaces that can be used in extended range telepresence (*exoskeletons* and *mobile haptic interfaces*), its limitations and drawbacks led us to design a new type of interface, called a *semi-mobile haptic interface*, which aims at combining the advantages and avoiding the limitations of the previous interfaces.

The first part of this thesis is dedicated to navigation assistance algorithms, whereas the second part is dedicated to the design and control of the new semi-mobile haptic interface. Both parts are tightly connected by the transformation of position and haptic information between the target and user environments, which is the focus of Chapter 3. The overall concept of the telepresence system with haptic guidance is presented in that chapter. Motion Compression's contribution to navigation assistance is explained, and the effects of the transformation caused by Motion Compression on perceived haptic information are analyzed. Since these effects increase with the difference of curvature between the desired target path and the path that the user actually covers, this difference should be kept as small as possible.

In Chapter 4, the *Plenhaptic Guidance Function* (PHGF) is presented. This guidance function systematically takes knowledge about the context information in the target environment and the intended goal in order to infer the optimal target path towards the goal. The PHGF allows navigation assistance in environments of arbitrary size for both typical navigation tasks: *path-directed guidance* and *goal-directed* guidance. The context information, which consists on the position of the intended goals and the geometries of the target and the user environment, is assumed to be given. The PHGF allows the guidance to pursue simultaneous (or equally probable) goals. To the best of the authors knowledge, this is the first guidance function that allows this.

The user is effectively guided by rendering the PHGF with the force control methods presented in Chapter 5. Two force control methods for intuitive user guidance are presented, *active* and *passive* ones, and these two can be combined. In this chapter, performance measures for wide-area haptic guidance have been defined and an experimental evaluation has been performed in order to identify the most adequate force control methods and parameters for both *path-directed* and *goal-directed* navigation tasks.

The concept and the control scheme for a generic SMHI is presented in Chapter 6. A variable directional admittance model is used to display defined forces and to render the PHGF. Owing to the new *mirror configuration* of the SMHI, a simple prepositioning algorithm affords the user an unrestricted workspace. The effects of the human arm impedance and the manipulator dynamics on the stability of the haptic interface were investigated in order to provide some guidelines on the interface design and the proper parametrization of the admittance control.

The new mechanical design for the SMHI with *mirror configuration* is presented in Chapter 7. The new prototype was designed to overcome the drawbacks of the previous SMHI with *frontal configuration*, namely: difficult prepositioning, deficient workspace utilization, poor force display quality, and a need for improvement with regards to user safety. The new haptic manipulator has two DOFs and a lightweight mechanical design. It is situated atop the user, and the planar workspace of the manipulator reflects the user's arm planar workspace. The new design was extensively evaluated to determine its specifications with regard to dexterous workspace, output capability, and backdrivability. An experimental evaluation of the whole system has been carried out in order to investigate the benefits of haptic navigation assistance in a very large telepresent scenario.

Finally, the main results of this thesis are summarized in Chapter 8. In addition, several extension points that are worth being considered in future research are presented.

2. State of the Art

The goal of this chapter is to present related work in the areas of haptic guidance and haptic interfaces and to analyze the usability of the existing approaches for *extended range telepresence*. Section 2.1 presents the principles and existing methods of haptic guidance, as well as the classification of those principles and methods. Although much work has been done in recent years in the field of haptic guidance, very few methods are adequate for the intuitive guidance of a human operator in arbitrarily large target environments.

Analogously, with exception of some interfaces presented in Section 2.2, most haptic interfaces that have been developed thus far are adequate neither for extended range telepresence nor for wide-area haptic guidance. In this work, a novel type of haptic interface specifically designed for extended range telepresence is presented.

2.1. Haptic Guidance Methods

Haptic guidance or assistance is known as the display of haptic information (force and motion guidance commands) that helps the user perform a task. The general objectives of haptic guidance are: to enhance performance; to reduce workload; and to improve skill acquisition. Haptic guidance methods have achieved good results in increasing accuracy and reducing execution time of manipulation tasks in which the user does not move.

Haptic assistance can be used for two types of robotic manipulation systems: *collaborative manipulation systems* and *teleoperation systems* [5].

Most applications of haptic guidance are in the field of collaborative manipulation, in which the manipulator and the user are physically in contact and perform the manipulation task together. However, many of the guidance methods can be transferred to teleoperation tasks. Applications of haptic guidance include:

- surgery applications to assist the surgeon in his/her work [61, 75, 86, 99];

- assembly tasks with high loads to lighten the weight and inertia of the object being manipulated [94];

- training of high-precision and/or high speed motions that make the task difficult to perform and to learn [90, 96, 98];

- and gaming applications to enhance human performance, e.g., [36].

Less work has been done in the domain of wide-area haptic navigation assistance. The Care-Robot, developed by [42] to assist the elderly in walking, can autonomously detect and avoid obstacles. A similar approach that also includes autonomous collision avoidance is used in [41] for shopping assistance with the Interactive Behavior Operated Shopping Trolley (InBOT). Furthermore, the robot-trolley is equipped with additional autonomous modes that can be activated by user voice commands. The two systems share two key features: the need for explicit commands from the user, as well as the presence of an autonomous robot whose trajectory is corrected by the user's input forces. By contrast, in our telepresence system, the operator has the ultimate control over the teleoperator's motion and velocity.

A survey of existing guidance approaches (also known as *task-related controllers*) is presented in [89]. Guidance approaches can be classified into three groups that differ from each other in two ways: first, in the amount of control the operator has; and second, in their software and hardware requirements. These three groups, which are explained in detail in following subsections, are:

- record and replay strategies,

- shared control and master-slave mappings;

- and virtual fixtures.

2.1.1. Record and Replay Strategies

Record and replay strategies for collaborative manipulation are inspired in teaching by demonstration: the dynamics of an expert is recorded while performing the task, and is then played back to the novice to assist learning. Some examples of this haptic guidance approach are found in [33, 40, 65]. The main drawback of the record and replay training scheme is that it does not account for differences due to user-specific dynamics or performance.

An assistance concept that is similar to record and replay strategies, but that is found in the field of teleoperation, is the *hidden robot concept* by [64]. The assistance consists of two steps here: First, the task is easily performed by the user in a virtual environment; and second, the task is reproduced by the teleoperator in the real target environment. The main challenge consists in the transformation of human actions into robot controller commands. By using the hidden robot concept, the master subsystem is decoupled from the slave subsystem, resulting in two closed-loop systems with high bandwidth and in an intuitive task execution for the user.

In both schemes, the user has little or no control over the task. Moreover, the requirements on the system are very high. On the one hand, the target environment must be precisely known in advance. On the other hand, the teleoperator has to be able to deal with unforeseen events on his own, e.g., by means of sensors and autonomous obstacle avoidance methods, since the operator will not perceive changed situations in the real environment.

2.1.2. Shared Control

There are different definitions of shared control in the literature. In typical shared control paradigms, the robot autonomously undertakes low-level tasks as obstacle avoidance, whereas the operator undertakes the high-level decisions [44]. According to other definitions of shared control, the operator is supported in performing the task by additional control actions from an autonomously acting agent. Shared control is used for both collaborative manipulation and teleoperation. While control is shared between the human and the autonomous robot in a collaborative manipulation task, in teleoperation the control over the teleoperator is shared between an autonomously acting controller and the human operator.

A few remarks and observations concerning shared control for collaborative tasks are stated here:

- In [85, 98], shared control takes information of the system dynamics into account so as to calculate additional forces that are added to the user's force on the master site in order to suppress undesired motions. Positive results were achieved in the performance of high dynamic tasks.

- In [45], the proposed shared control for virtual driving assistance is a virtual spring that depends on the orientation error of the steering wheel. In this work the controller is responsible for keeping to the lane, whereas the human operator is responsible for avoiding obstacles.

- While interacting with the Care-Robot [42] or the InBOT Robot [41] mentioned above, the user assumes part of the control over the direction of motion or velocity, whereas the autonomous controller takes care of obstacle avoidance. The final velocity of the robot is the weighted sum of the input velocities of user and controller.

- A partial leader or follower behavior is considered in the framework by [32]. The human can behave with a proportion $\alpha \in [0,1]$ as follower (of the robot) and $(1 - \alpha)$ as leader. The robot will apply a mirrored version of the human behavior.

In collaborative tasks, the user perceives the corrective actions from the autonomous robot because both are physically in contact. However, this is not the case in teleoperation when the user and the autonomous controller share control over the slave robot, as in [44]. In this case, the user's and the slave's motion may differ without the user realizing it. Some approaches solve this problem by signaling to the user that the controller is taking control of the task, e.g. by means of LEDs or acoustic signals.

In the literature, we also find some work in which the shared control is realized by letting the autonomous controller share control over the master robot with the user, and this alone dictates the motion of the slave. [21] proposes continuous haptic shared control for different types of motion: here, haptic cues are presented to the user in order to influence his/her motion. This kind of shared control cannot be distinguished from *virtual fixtures*, which are haptic signals superimposed onto haptic information from the target environment, and which are described in the next subsection.

Master-slave mappings as presented in [88, 124] are a mixture of both kinds of shared control: shared control of the slave and shared control of the master. The undesired displacement between the teleoperator's end-effector and a screw (the target object) is corrected by applying suitable velocity or force mappings between master and slave device: In position assistance mode, the position of the teleoperator is altered in such a way that a reaching movement towards the target is shifted in the direction of this target. In force assistance mode, a force is applied on the operator side to push the operator along the ideal target trajectory.

In all shared control approaches, the teleoperator requires additional sensors (e.g., distance sensors, a laser scanner, or an eye-in-hand camera). The information provided by these sensors together with knowledge about the task are used by the autonomous controller to assist the user.

2.1.3. Virtual Fixtures

Virtual fixtures were first defined by [105] as perceptual overlays to improve performance. Virtual fixtures are added to help a human perform a task by limiting the human operator's movement to restricted regions and/or influencing his/her movement along desired paths. In contrast to shared control and record and replay strategies, in teleoperation with virtual fixtures, the user has the ultimate control on the task, and position deviations between master and slave devices cannot occur.

As mentioned above, the frontier between virtual fixtures and shared control for collaborative tasks is quite diffuse, since the operator and the autonomous robot are directly coupled. In each case, guidance with virtual fixtures is categorized as a *gross guidance* paradigm [98], because guidance signals and target forces are summed up in the haptic device. Two other guidance paradigms are *temporally separated assistance*, where the guidance signals are desynchronized from the target information, and *spatially separated assistance*, where the guidance signals are applied on another channel or other part of the user's body. In the user study presented in [98], the *gross guidance* paradigm showed significantly better performance than *temporally separated assistance* and *spatially separated assistance* in a target-hitting task.

Virtual fixtures also appear in the literature under other names, such as *constrained Cartesian motion* in [38], *haptically augmented teleoperation* in [120], or *virtual mechanisms* in [59]. Virtual fixtures can help the user follow a trajectory, in which case they are called *guiding virtual fixtures*; or they can help the user avoid certain regions, as in the case of *forbidden-region virtual fixtures* [4]. Fig. 2.1 illustrates these concepts. Furthermore, virtual fixtures can be applied to impedance-controlled or to admittance-controlled robotic systems [6]. Visual-based virtual fixtures implemented in admittance-controlled cooperative systems can be found in [1, 17–19, 70, 77, 78, 96]. According to [3] virtual fixtures can be classified as *active* and *passive*. According to this definition, virtual fixtures are passive if they are only able to restrict, and not generate, the end-effector's motion.

(a) (b)

Fig. 2.1.: Concept of virtual fixtures [4]. (a) Guiding virtual fixtures assist in guiding the robot along desired paths. (b) Forbidden-region virtual fixtures help keep the robot out of forbidden regions.

Virtual fixtures require knowledge about the task and the remote environment. The main challenges for applying virtual fixtures are the choice of the right fixture, the optimal trade-off between entirely human-commanded and purely computer-controlled operation, and the recognition of task primitives [89]. In summary, the adaptation of the fixtures to context information about the task and the user's intention is still an open research question in the design of virtual fixtures.

2.1.4. Adaptation of Haptic Assistance

Hidden Markov models (HMM) are trainable statistical models with unobservable states, which have often been used for the purpose of recognizing simple and general task segments called primitives [1, 31, 70, 76]. The recognition of task primitives is important to make virtual fixtures adaptable and generalizable to different tasks. However, with HMM, the guidance in a modified environment or towards alternative goals requires the laborious task of generating and training new models.

Potential field methods have been widely used for path planning of autonomous robots and obstacle avoidance [8, 63, 126]. The main advantage of potential field methods is that they are easy to compute and can manage context information by superimposing several geometric shapes [63]. The user is guided in the target environment by using repulsive force fields around the obstacles to be avoided and attractive force fields around target regions. However, by using such force fields, the user permanently perceives a force in the direction of the force field and is then constrained to walk towards the direction dictated by the force field.

[104] and [34] demonstrate efficient methods to compute a motion plan that provides the direction to be followed to reach the goal from any free configuration of the configuration space. In [104], such a motion plan interleaves a sampling-based exploration of the configuration space with an efficient computation of harmonic functions. [34] proposes modifying a classic motion planning method, the rapidly-exploring random tree (RRT), so as to develop an interactive-RRT. The interactive-RRT takes the forces applied by the user into account in order to delimit the search for an efficient solution in the configuration space.

Another aspect in the design of haptic assistance is the consideration of the effect of guidance on the operator. The motion of the user should be constrained only if necessary. That is to say: Special care has to be taken in choosing the amount of assistance such that the operator neither feels too restricted in his/her actions nor becomes dependent on the assistance. For example, [55] proposes *progressive haptic guidance* for training: Here, the guidance gain decreases when three successive trials have shown improvement in performance; and the corresponding gain increases when the performance decreases.

This thesis presents a new systematic approach to designing virtual fixtures that simultaneously considers both, contextual information from the environment, and several potential goal locations, so that the user can freely choose among these possible goals. The guidance fixtures in our approach are described by a dynamic guidance function called *Plenhaptic Guidance Function* (PHGF).

2.2. Haptic Interfaces

Haptic guidance can be achieved with passive robotic devices such as *collaborative robots* (cobots), e.g., the Scooter cobot [24]. Cobots [39, 94], which are typically used in collaborative assembly tasks, utilize the kinematic properties of the hardware design to create motion guidance. However, they are not suitable for displaying haptic information in extended range telepresence, because they would have to reorient its structure very quickly in order to display arbitrary forces from the target environment.

Although there are many commercially available interfaces (among others: PHANToM family [80], DELTA haptic device [43], the HapticMASTER [125], F3D-35, Virtuose 6D, INCA 6D of Haption, etc.), most of these haptic interfaces assume an immobile user and/or low output capability (velocity, acceleration, and/or force capability). A broader overview of haptic interfaces can be found in [26, 53, 79].

Haptic interfaces with a large workspace are presented in [22, 123]. However, in order to provide the user with realistic haptic information and haptic guidance in extended range telepresence, a haptic interface is required that simultaneously allows the user both unrestricted motion and display of defined forces. A survey of haptic interfaces for large-scale target environments is presented [72]. In this survey, different haptic display types are categorized according to their force reference system in: *unbased*, *body-based*, and *ground-based* haptic interfaces.

Unbased haptic interfaces use angular momentum for force reflection. Examples of this type are *jet-based* devices, such as the AirGlobe [46], and *gyro moment-based* devices, like the Gyro Moment Display [127]. However, these interfaces have a very small output capability and gyro moment-based devices can only display torques. A different approach is taken in body-based haptic interfaces, which use the operator's body as the force reaction base. Under this category, portable *exoskeletons* are the most common devices.

String-based interfaces [23] or *magnetic levitation-based* interfaces [16] fail under the ground-based haptic interfaces for large-scale target environments. The main problem of these interfaces is that force display quality, dexterity, and tracking accuracy degrade with increasing environment dimensions. More interesting are the recently developed *mobile haptic interfaces*, which combine desktop-sized workspace devices with mobile robot platforms.

2.2.1. Exoskeletons

Full-body exoskeletons have been developed to amplify human power and carry heavy loads [62]. Furthermore, arm exoskeletons are used as portable haptic interfaces and have almost unrestricted workspace, since the interface is carried along by the human operator. Examples of arm exoskeletons are found in [14, 15, 37, 93, 111, 119].

These interfaces also have advantages when there is a need to track the spatial configuration of the human arm for specific gesture recognition tasks or rehabilitation procedures [15]. They are also an effective solution in those cases in which the human operator must interact not only with remote/virtual objects, but also, at the same time, with real objects in the control space (e.g., a control panel).

However, the force feedback with these devices has some drawbacks. On the one hand, the maximum force that can be displayed by an exoskeleton is limited by the weight of the system, which must be carried by the user. On the other hand, the human operator feels the reaction torques generated during the application of forces, since the base of the interface is situated on the user's body, so that the display of high forces would be unpleasant for the user. Both effects can lead to a reduction of the immersion in the target environment. However, the main drawback of this interface is the unrealistic display of forces that result from the contact with grounded virtual objects, e.g., virtual walls [100].

2.2.2. Mobile Haptic Interfaces

Mobile haptic interfaces [11, 35, 82, 84] are usually desktop haptic devices mounted on a mobile platform. Whereas the first mobile haptic interfaces suffered from a small output capability, recently developed mobile haptic interfaces can display high forces by mounting a larger haptic manipulator on the mobile platform, as in [92].

Although these interfaces are suitable for extended range telepresence, they have some drawbacks that are inherent to the use of a mobile platform. These drawbacks are the difficult position control, especially by nonholonomic platforms and the inherent compliance of the platform's wheels, which reduces the force display quality [81]. Moreover, since the transparency of the haptic display is largely dependent of the localization quality of the platform [82], the combination of odometry and dynamic localization methods is needed in order to achieve the required high relative accuracy together with sufficient bandwidth.

2.2.3. Semi-mobile Haptic Interfaces

The drawbacks of exoskeletons and mobile haptic interfaces led us to develop a new type of haptic interface, called *semi-mobile haptic interfaces* (SMHI). They consist of a mobile haptic manipulator (HM) and a grounded prepositioning unit (PPU). The grounded PPU moves the manipulator all over the user environment. Because the PPU is grounded, it can be constructed very rigidly and support high forces. By choosing a Cartesian kinematics for the PPU, the position control and the localization of the interface are straightforward. In [106, 145], we presented the first prototype of a semi-mobile haptic interface. Fig. 2.2 illustrates the concept of the SMHI.

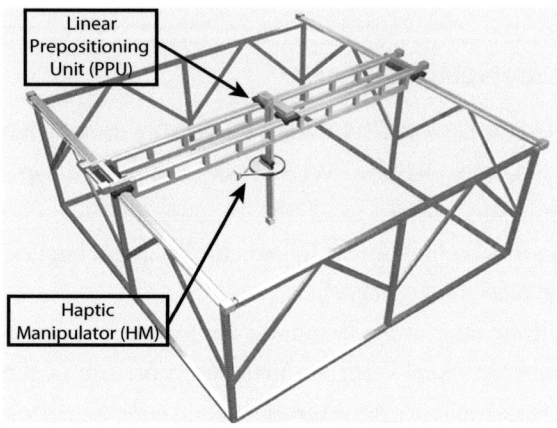

Fig. 2.2.: Model of an exemplary Semi-mobile Haptic Interface.

In this work, the design and the control of a new ergonomic configuration for the semi-mobile haptic interface are presented. The realization of the new configuration with a lightweight haptic manipulator has made it possible to improve the mobility of the user, the maneuverability of the device, the ease of operation, and user safety in the user environment, and also to increase force feedback fidelity.

2.3. Summary

In this chapter, existing approaches related to the two core topics of this thesis, wide-area haptic guidance and haptic interaction, have been presented and the possibility to apply them to extended range telepresence has been investigated, in particular so as to offer the user consistent multi-modal feedback from the target environment.

Some of the investigated guidance methods, most notably virtual fixtures, provide the highest level of user control, since the teleoperator precisely follows the motion of the user. Virtual fixtures will therefore be used for guidance in extended range telepresence. However, only *ad-hoc* solutions exist to adapt virtual fixtures to changed conditions in the target environment. A novel algorithm will be presented, that systematically considers context information from the target environment, and that leaves the user enough motion freedom to choose between different possible goals.

Finally, the drawbacks of existing haptic interfaces have been explained. In order to overcome these drawbacks, a new type of haptic interface, called semi-mobile haptic interface (SMHI), is used. In conjunction with Motion Compression [83], semi-mobile haptic interfaces enable the human operator to haptically explore arbitrarily large target environments.

3. Integration of Haptic Information into Extended Range Telepresence

In *extended range telepresence*, the feeling of presence is not only achieved by visual and acoustic sensory information recorded from the *target environment* and presented to the user on an immersive display, but also by proprioception, i.e., the sense of one's own motion in the target environment, which is especially important for human navigation and path finding [29, 95, 117].

Without further processing of the motion information, the motion of the human operator is restricted to the size of the *user environment*. To allow the exploration of arbitrarily large target environments, while walking in the limited user environment, Motion Compression [83, 108, 109] is used. While preserving the length of the path and the turning angles, Motion Compression curves the desired path in the target environment, the *target path*, until it fits into the limited user environment and then guides the user on this *user path* by taking advantage of the fact that humans do not notice small inconsistencies between the displayed and the perceived path curvature during locomotion [83]. As a result, in extended range telepresence, the visual channel not only serves the purpose of displaying the target environment, but also that of guiding the user to remain within the limits of the user environment. Fig. 3.1 illustrates the concept of this information augmentation.

The additional use of haptic information in extended range telepresence, which is in any case indispensable for perceiving interactions in the target environment more realistically, offers a very intuitive channel for guiding the user more reliably not only in the user environment but also in the target

25

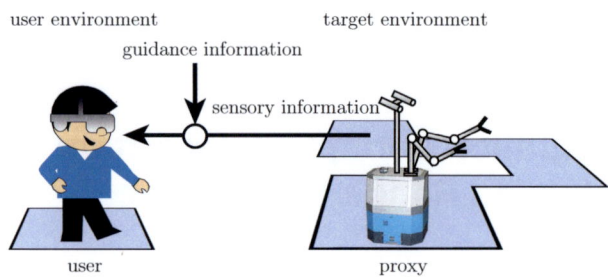

Fig. 3.1.: Superposition of information in extended range telepresence.

environment by using the same augmentation scheme. However, none of the existing haptic guidance methods in the literature are suitable for guiding the user in an arbitrarily large target environment from a smaller user environment. Furthermore, most of existing methods rely on a predefined path or a set of paths, and cannot easily be modified by taking the user's intention into account.

This chapter presents a novel framework that takes advantage of the properties of Motion Compression for wide-area haptic guidance and still leaves the user the possibility of changing his/her goal and path. In order to understand the benefits of this framework, first, the principles of Motion Compression will be reviewed, and the framework in which Motion Compression is embedded will be then presented. The effects of Motion Compression on perceived haptic information from the target environment will also be analyzed.

3.1. Overall Control of Telepresence System with Haptic Guidance

In the extended range telepresence system with haptic feedback, there are two control loops closed around the user (Fig. 3.2(a)):

- the control loop for goal-oriented telepresent navigation, which is based on visual and proprioceptive stimuli;

- and the control loop for telepresent manipulation with haptic information, based on visual and haptic stimuli.

In such a system, the position of the human operator is tracked in order to achieve wide-area motion. A large-scale acoustic tracking system is used for this purpose [20, 143]. The pose data are transmitted through the communication channel to the proxy, i.e., an avatar in a virtual target environment, and a teleoperator consisting of a mobile platform and a pan-tilt camera head in a real target environment. The motion of the user is then replicated by the proxy. In a real target environment, the camera head records images of the target environment from the teleoperator's perspective and sends them to the human operator, where they are displayed on a head-mounted display (HMD). This visual information, complemented by proprioceptive perception, gives the user a realistic feedback for self-localization and influences his/her motion. In this way, the first control loop for goal-oriented navigation is closed on the user. Please note that the same procedure is valid for a virtual target environment.

As already mentioned, without Motion Compression, the motion of the user is restricted to the size of the user environment. Motion Compression provides a linear time-and-position-dependent transformation between both environments and augments the visual information displayed to the human operator, so that the human operator does not leave the user environment while walking towards his target into the target environment.

At the same time, the user's hand is attached in the user environment to a haptic interface, an input-output device that is controlled to display the forces acting on the end-effector of the proxy (in a virtual target environment the contact forces are calculated by haptic rendering). The haptic device also measures the motion of the user's hand in the user environment. This motion data is sent to the target environment and replicated by the end-effector of the proxy. In this way, the second loop, the closed-loop for haptic manipulation, is closed.

In the telepresence system with haptic guidance there is a third control loop acting on the user (Fig. 3.2(b)). This control loop integrates visual, proprioceptive, and haptic stimuli and governs, together with the visual control loop, the navigation of the human operator in the target environment. It is therefore essential that both visual and haptic navigation loops provide consistent information. The closed-loop for haptic guidance works as follows:

First, regarding the current pose of the proxy and context information from the target environment (e.g., the positions of desired goals and obstacles), a desired target path and the instantaneous preferred direction of motion in the target environment is inferred. Second, Motion Compression transforms the desired target path, and thus also the guidance direction, in the user environment. The guidance information is then rendered (transformed into haptic commands) and added to the contact information from the target environment. The resultant haptic information is displayed to the user through the haptic interface.

On the one hand, the user is able to discern the preferred direction of motion from the rendered guidance information; and on the other hand, the user knows or infers his/her current position from the gathered visual and proprioceptive information. Then, the user uses the information about preferred direction and the self-localization information in order to plan and execute his/her motion, not only of his/her hand but also of his/her body. Finally, the new user's hand and head positions, which are registered by the haptic device and the tracking system, respectively, are transformed with Motion Compression and sent to the target environment via the communication channel, closing thus the third control loop. A simplified representation of the complex sensory, actuatory, and cognitive human processes taking place during haptic guidance is depicted in Fig. 3.3.

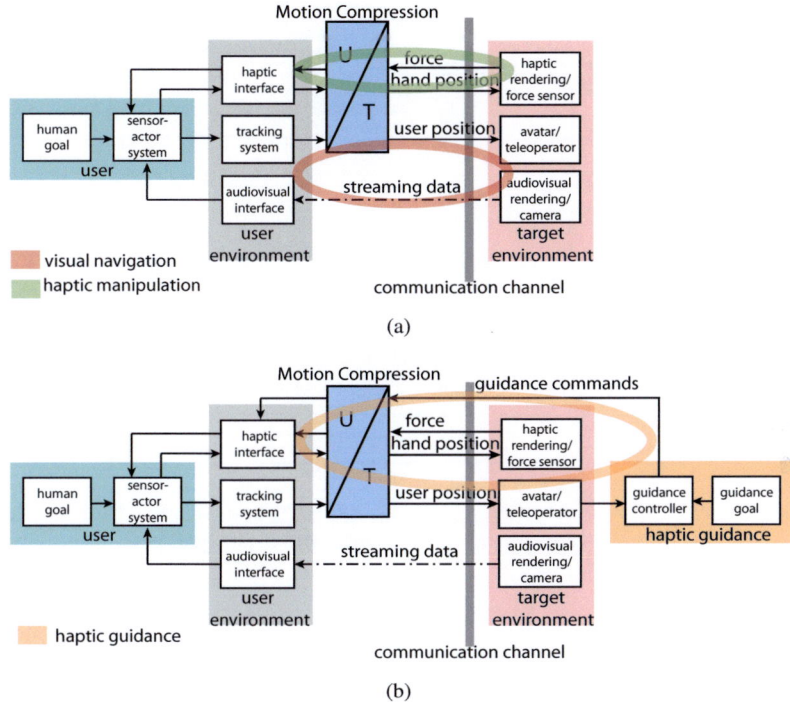

Fig. 3.2.: Data flow in the extended range telepresent system, (a) with haptic feedback, and (b) with additional haptic guidance.

3.2. Algorithmic Framework

Fig. 3.4 illustrates the algorithmic framework of the proposed wide-area haptic guidance. The instantaneous transformation provided by Motion Compression, which relates the position of the user in the target environment and in the user environment, is an essential part of the proposed wide-area haptic guidance.

In order to allow the user to modify his/her plan and change his/her goal, a *goal prediction* algorithm that estimates the user's goal out of a set of possible goals is necessary. For example, in our previous work [110], a

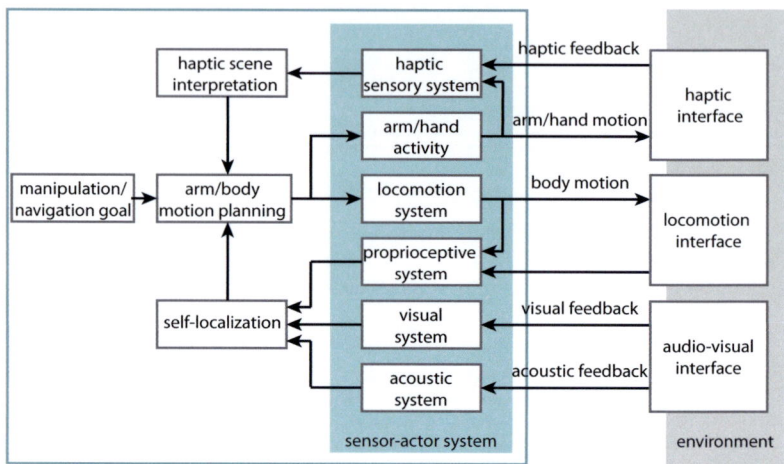

Fig. 3.3.: Abstract representation of sensory, actuatory, and cognitive processes of the user in extended range telepresence with haptic guidance.

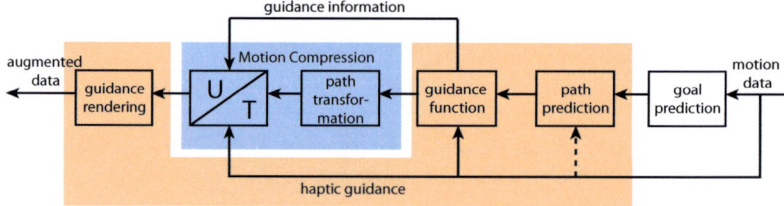

Fig. 3.4.: Algorithmic framework of the proposed wide-area haptic guidance.

stochastic prediction of way-points for extended range telepresence applications is presented. However, any method for goal prediction can be used in this module. In this thesis, the predicted goal, or set of equally probable goals, is assumed to be given.

The selected goal and the information about the obstacles in the target environment are then used to calculate the desired path within the *path prediction* module. As it will be explained in Chapter 4, there are two possible ways to calculate this path, which rely on two typical human locomotion models. The choice of one of them depends on the desired mode of haptic guidance, either *path-directed* or *goal-directed*. In the case of a *path-directed guidance*, the path is calculated once for a selected goal, and the user is guided to walk along this path. In case of a *goal-directed guidance*, the path prediction is actualized at each time step with the current user's position, so that the optimal path towards the selected goal is recalculated from the current user's position.

The guidance function module is fed with the desired path. This module calculates the preferred direction of motion and the amount of guidance at each direction by means of the *Plenhaptic Guidance Function* (PHGF), which will be described in Chapter 4.

In the *path transformation* module of Motion Compression, the *user path*, which fits into the user environment, is calculated. The resultant user path has the same length as the original *target path* and the minimum difference of curvature. The optimal user path is the solution of a nonlinear optimization problem with boundary conditions, which has no analytic solution in the general case. Therefore, the infinite-dimensional optimization problem is transformed into a finite-dimensional optimization problem by representing the paths as the sum of circular arcs with different curvatures [106]. For more details on the path transformation provided by Motion Compression, the reader is referred to [81, 106].

In the next module of Motion Compression, called *user guidance*, the user is visually guided along the user path (otherwise the user would leave the user environment) by means of an adequate transformation of the proxy's pose. Whereas the user walks in the user environment, the pose of the proxy is so altered, that the user perceives an orientation error towards his goal that he/she tries to compensate for, according to the human navigation models [81, 109]. In this way, the user is visually guided on the intended user path. The result of this step is an instantaneous position-dependent transformation (or mapping) between the target and user environments. This transformation can be used to exchange not only the user position, but also the user's hand position and force vectors between the user and target environments. However, the visual guidance provided by Motion Compression alone cannot prevent the user from leaving the user environment, e.g., if he/she deviates orthogonally from the user path.

Finally, the haptic guidance information is transformed with the inverse of the instantaneous mapping, and the guidance information is rendered, i.e., transformed into haptic signals that augment the haptic information from the target environment. Two complementary methods used to render the guidance information are presented in Chapter 5.

Please note that in the case of path-directed haptic guidance, the path transformation only has to be performed once at the beginning. In this case, the path transformation is called *static path transformation*. In the case of goal-directed haptic guidance, the path prediction depends on the user's position, and the calculated transformed path begins at the current position, called the *planning reference point*. In this case, the path transformation is called *dynamic path transformation* and an *incremental user guidance* is used, which considerably simplifies the calculation of the mapping between user and target environments. The calculation of the mapping between user and target environments is described in next section.

3.3. Transformation between User and Target Environments

The output of the user guidance module is an instantaneous transformation that relates the current user's pose to the desired pose of the proxy in the target environment that makes the user walk on the intended target path and the corresponding user path. Therefore, the calculation of the transformation is based on the predicted target path, the corresponding "compressed" user path, and the current pose of the user, which is tracked in the user environment.

3.3.1. Calculation of Transformation

For the calculation of the transformation, it is convenient to express the pose of user and proxy as a homogeneous transformation between the local coordinate systems S_{HU} and S_{HT} and the world coordinate systems S_{OU} and S_{OT}. The transformation

$$^{OU}\mathbf{T}_{HU} = \begin{bmatrix} \cos(\phi_U) & -\sin(\phi_U) & x_U \\ \sin(\phi_U) & \cos(\phi_U) & y_U \\ 0 & 0 & 1 \end{bmatrix} \tag{3.1}$$

describes the pose of the user. Analogously, the pose of the proxy is represented by $^{OT}\mathbf{T}_{HT}$.

Once the transformation between the user environment and the target environment $^{OT}\mathbf{T}_{OU}$ has been calculated, the sought pose of the proxy $^{OT}\mathbf{T}_{HT}$ can be calculated as

$$^{OT}\mathbf{T}_{HT} = {}^{OT}\mathbf{T}_{OU} \cdot {}^{OU}\mathbf{T}_{HU} . \tag{3.2}$$

In order to calculate the transformation $^{OT}\mathbf{T}_{OU}$, it is convenient to represent the pose of user and proxy in curvilinear coordinate systems $\tilde{S}_U$, $\tilde{S}_T$, with the coordinates s and n (cf. Fig. 3.5). s_U is the covered way along the user path, n_U is the orthogonal distance to the path, and θ_U is the orientation of the user with respect to the user path. The same applies for the coordinates s_T, n_T, and θ_T with respect to the target path.

In the curvilinear coordinate systems $\tilde{S}_U$ and $\tilde{S}_T$, the necessary and sufficient conditions for the conservation of length and turning angles are given by

$$\begin{aligned} s_T &= s_U , \\ n_T &= n_U , \text{ and} \\ \theta_T &= \theta_U . \end{aligned} \tag{3.3}$$

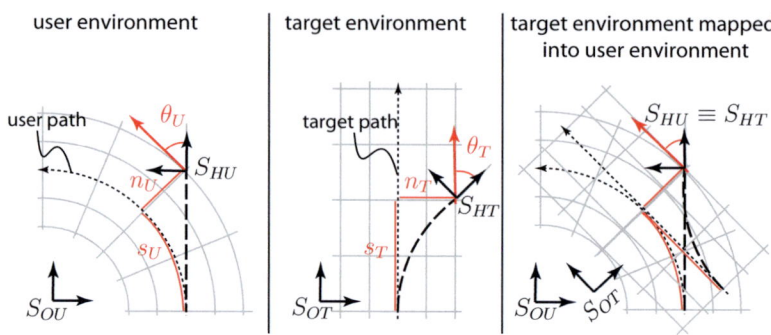

Fig. 3.5.: User position in both curvilinear coordinate systems defined by n, s, θ.

From the mentioned conditions, the relative poses of user and proxy relative to their respective paths are identical, so that $^{HT}\tilde{\mathbf{T}}_{HU}$ is the identity matrix. Given the pose of the user in the user environment, the transformation that describes the pose of the user with respect to the user path $\tilde{s}_U$, i.e., $^{HU}\tilde{\mathbf{T}}_{OU}$, has to first be calculated. To do this, the projection of the user position on the calculated user path, the so-called *planning reference point*, is calculated. Then s_U, n_U, and θ_U, and the corresponding $^{OU}\tilde{\mathbf{T}}_{HU}$ can be inferred.

The curvilinear transformation in the target environment $^{OT}\tilde{\mathbf{T}}_{HT}$ is straightforward by using the length-preserving and angle-preserving conditions together with the predicted target path. This transformation results

$$
^{OT}\tilde{\mathbf{T}}_{HT} = \begin{bmatrix} \cos(\varphi_T + \theta_T) & -\sin(\varphi_T + \theta_T) & c_{x,T} - n_T \cdot \sin(\varphi_T) \\ \sin(\varphi_T + \theta_T) & \cos(\varphi_T + \theta_T) & c_{y,T} + n_T \cdot \cos(\varphi_T) \\ 0 & 0 & 1 \end{bmatrix} , \quad (3.4)
$$

where $\varphi_T(s_T)$ is the angle of the tangent of the target path at s_T and $\underline{c}_T(s_T)$ is the Cartesian position on the target path at s_T.

Finally, the sought transformation can be calculated

$$
^{OT}\mathbf{T}_{OU} = {}^{OT}\tilde{\mathbf{T}}_{HT} \cdot {}^{HU}\tilde{\mathbf{T}}_{OU} . \quad (3.5)
$$

3.3.2. Incremental Calculation

The transformation calculated as above is not practical for dynamic Motion Compression, in which the path prediction and the path transformation are performed at each time step, since this would require the storage of a huge history of covered path segments. Therefore, an incremental calculation is used, one in which the final transformation is the product of the transformation in the last step $^{OT}\mathbf{T}_{OU,k-1}$ multiplied by the change in the transformation due to the latest user motion $\mathbf{T}_{ink,k}$ as

$$^{OT}\mathbf{T}_{OU,k} = {}^{OT}\mathbf{T}_{OU,k-1} \cdot \mathbf{T}_{ink,k} \,. \tag{3.6}$$

For the calculation of $\mathbf{T}_{ink,k}$, only the path segment that begins at the *planning reference point* is used. From this point, the increments Δs_U, Δn_U, $\Delta \theta_U$ are used for the calculation of the incremental transformation analogously to (3.4).

3.3.3. Properties of Transformation

$^{OT}\mathbf{T}_{OU}$ describes the instantaneous location of the target environment relative to the user environment. It can be interpreted as the linearization of the non-linear mapping between the user's and the proxy's positions at the operating point, i.e., the user's current position [81]. This transformation remains constant if the position along the paths (s_U or s_T) does not change, for example, if the user only rotates or moves orthogonally to the path.

When the user moves along the path, $^{OT}\mathbf{T}_{OU}$ changes and the user perceives the target environment transformed with $^{OT}\mathbf{T}_{OU}^{-1}$, which corresponds to the rolling motion of the target path on the user path. The rotational velocity of this rolling motion w_{UT} depends on the curvature difference between the user and the target path $\Delta \kappa = \kappa_U - \kappa_T$, and the velocity of the user along the path $\frac{ds}{dt}$ as

$$w_{UT} = (\kappa_U - \kappa_T) \frac{ds}{dt} \, . \tag{3.7}$$

The desired length-preserving and angle-preserving properties are satisfied on account of the transformation between curvilinear coordinate systems. However, this transformation originates, for an infinitesimal motion along the path ds, a length error Δr in the Cartesian coordinate system

$$\frac{d\Delta r}{ds} = n \cdot \Delta \kappa \, , \tag{3.8}$$

where n is the orthogonal deviation from the user path, so that length preservation is valid only for $n = 0$ and/or $\Delta \kappa = 0$

The instantaneous transformation $^{OT}\mathbf{T}_{OU}$ can be used to transform every position from the user environment into the target environment. This is particularly valid for the hand position, so that the relative location between the user's head and the user's hand is preserved, and the user perceives the end-effector of the proxy in the position dictated by his efferent subjective perception.

Analogously, all interesting points in the target environment are transformed back into the user environment with the inverse transformation $^{OT}\mathbf{T}_{OU}^{-1}$. The haptic information (interaction force, guidance force, and guidance direction) is transformed as well with the inverse transformation, in such a way that the instantaneous transformation of haptic vectors is a rotation around the vertical axis. Since the transformation is instantaneously angle-preserving, the user perceives the force acting in the same relative direction with respect to his body in both environments. However, due to the difference of path curvature in both environments, some inconsistencies in the perceived haptic information arise, which are discussed in next section.

3.4. Effects of Transformation on Haptic Information

The haptic guidance information, as will be described in Chapter 4, depends only on the relative position between user and reference path. Since the normal and tangent direction are coincident in both environments, the transformation provides consistent guidance information in both environments. Namely, haptic guidance with static Motion Compression is equivalent to guiding the user on the one-time predicted user path. However, by using dynamic Motion Compression, the user is guided back to an instantaneous user path that depends on the current user's position, and that cannot be predicted in advance.

Due to the properties of the transformation, the length preservation is valid only for motions along the user path. However, the user's hand position normally deviates from the path, so that the lengths of the paths covered by user's hand and the proxy's hand are generally different.

Example 3.1 Straight Target Path

Consider the following: The user walks with his right arm extended along a straight path of length $2\pi R_H$ in the target environment. Let's assume for simplicity that the compressed user path is a circular path of the same length as the target path. Whereas the proxy's hand (or end-effector) follows a straight path of the same length $2\pi R_H$ in the target environment, the user's hand covers a circular path of length $2\pi R_E$ that is concentric to the user path but has a bigger radius R_E. The difference between the distances covered by the proxy's hand and the user's hand is $2\pi(R_E - R_H)$, $R_E - R_H$ being the normal distance from the user's hand to the user path, in this case, the arm's length. ∎

For the same reason, the mapping of rigid bodies into the target environment has to be done by using the pose of the centroid (center of the area) of the rigid body as the center of the transformation and then rotating the rigid body as a whole with the transformation. Otherwise, by transforming each point of the body separately into the target environment, the transformed object would become distorted.

In the same way, because of the difference of curvature between the target and user paths, the user will perceive straight objects in the target environment as curved. This is analyzed in the following two situations, situations wherein these inconsistencies affect the perceived haptic information.

Carrying an Object in the Target Environment

From the properties of the transformation formulated in (3.8), the magnitude of the velocity of a carried object in the user environment $v_{0,U}$ satisfies

$$v_{0,U} = v_{0,T}(1 + n \cdot \Delta\kappa) , \tag{3.9}$$

where $v_{0,T}$ is the magnitude of the velocity of the object in the target environment, n is the signed normal distance between this object and the user path, and $\Delta\kappa$ is the instantaneous curvature difference between the user and the target path from Section 3.3.3. The same relation also applies for the velocity of the user's hand or the velocity of a person rigidly coupled to the user.

Please note that if the velocity of the object were the same in the user and the target environment, the object would move slower than the proxy in the target environment. As a result, the user, who is the center of the transformation, would visually perceive that he/she leaves the object behind him/her in the target environment. The same problem occurs when two persons manipulate an object together. Although their velocities are equal in the target environment, one person must be faster than the other in the user environment in order to preserve their relative orientation in both environments.

In order to quantify the quality of the force feedback in telepresence systems, Lawrence [73] formulated the *transparency condition* in the frequency domain as the equality of the impedance transmitted to the operator

Z_U and the impedance of the environment Z_T together with the equality of master and slave velocities as

$$Z_U \equiv \frac{F_U}{V_U} = Z_T \equiv \frac{F_T}{V_T} \text{ and } V_U = V_T, \tag{3.10}$$

where the capital letters are the Laplace-transformed variables, and where F stands for force and V stands for velocity. In practice, perfectly transparent telepresence cannot be achieved due to sample-hold effects and dynamic effects between the master and the slave, but rather in extended range telepresence, since the velocities of the master and the slave generally differ. Perfect force fidelity as defined in [73] therefore cannot be achieved even under the assumption of ideal conditions.

Furthermore, when carrying an object there is also an inconsistency between the displayed impedance in both environments. This happens because the same force magnitude is applied in both environments whereas the velocity of the object in the user environment is larger (if n is positive) or smaller (if n is negative) than the velocity in the target environment. In this case, the apparent impedance becomes

$$Z_U = Z_T \frac{V_T}{V_U}, \tag{3.11}$$

and according to this, when the impedance is reduced to a mass, the apparent mass becomes

$$m_{0,U} = m_{0,T}(1 + n \cdot \Delta \kappa)^{-1}, \tag{3.12}$$

where $m_{0,T}$ is the target mass, and $m_{0,U}$ in the mass perceived in the user environment.

Although perfect force fidelity cannot be achieved in practice, research in human perception has shown that if the difference between haptic signals is below a certain value, the user cannot distinguish between the different signals [26,60]. The detection threshold, called the *Just Noticeable Difference*

(JND), usually follows, for most senses, a linear relationship called Weber's Law. That is to say: the JND is proportional to the perceived signal. Investigations of Jones and Hunter [60] indicate a JND for the perception of motion with the arm $JND_v \approx 8\%$. Beauregard and Srinivasan [12] identified a JND for mass at the arm/forearm $JND_m \approx 35\%$.

Example 3.2 Curvature Difference for Velocity Detection Threshold JND_v

The proportional difference between user and target velocities should be

$$\frac{\|v_{0,U} - v_{0,T}\|}{v_{0,T}} \times 100 = \|n \cdot \Delta\kappa\| \times 100 \leq JND_v \ , \tag{3.13}$$

so that the user does not perceive the velocity inconsistency. Assuming a typical distance between the user's hand and the user path $n = 0.5$ m, this would require that $\Delta\kappa \leq 0.16$ m^{-1}. This value is similar to the perception threshold of curvature deviation reported in [83]. With curvature differences lower than $\Delta\kappa = 0.1$ m^{-1}, persons are prone to make mistakes in deciding whether the user path is curved left or right. ∎

Example 3.3 Curvature Difference for Mass Detection Threshold JND_m

In the same way, the proportional difference between the perceived mass and the target mass should be

$$\frac{\|m_{0,U} - m_{0,T}\|}{m_{0,T}} \times 100 = \left\|\frac{n \cdot \Delta\kappa}{1 + n \cdot \Delta\kappa}\right\| \times 100 \leq JND_m \ , \tag{3.14}$$

so that the user does not perceive the inconsistencies. For the same normal distance $n = 0.5$ m, this is equivalent to $\Delta\kappa \leq 1.07$ m^{-1}. Please note that curvatures smaller than this value are easy to achieve for typical dimensions of the user environment, e.g., $4 \times 4\,\mathrm{m}^2$, and thus the user hardly notices the mass difference. ∎

Haptically Exploring a Straight Object in the Target Environment

A different effect arises when the haptic vectors are transformed with Motion Compression. Here, the user perceives a small inconsistency between the direction of the force in the target environment (as he/she visually perceives it) and the direction of the force that he/she actually feels. This occurs because the transformation changes when the user moves along the path independently of the hand position. Tan et al. [116] explored the threshold for force direction and found the threshold to be $\mathrm{JND}_\alpha = 0.58$ rad (33.23°), independent of the given reference force direction. In [97], the thresholds for force direction have been reported to be $\mathrm{JND}_\alpha = 0.47$ rad (26.92°) for motions toward the wrist, and $\mathrm{JND}_\alpha = 0.40$ rad (22.92°) for motions away from the wrist.

Example 3.4 Curvature Difference for Angle Detection Threshold JND_α

Consider the following: The user is walking parallel to a straight wall that he/she is in contact with, in the target environment. In the user environment, the user would perceive him/herself to be walking along a curved wall. The angle difference between the expected force and the felt force is proportional to the step length Δs and to the curvature difference $\Delta \kappa$

$$\Delta \alpha = \Delta s \cdot \Delta \kappa . \tag{3.15}$$

For a typical step length $\Delta s = 0.5$ m, the curvature difference should be $\Delta \kappa \leq 0.8\,\mathrm{m}^{-1}$ so that $\Delta \alpha$ is smaller than the lowest threshold. ∎

On the other hand, when the user moves a step Δs along his/her intended target path, an instantaneous deviation Δn from the user path occurs. Through the user guidance module, this deviation also results in the same deviation from the target path, which has to be compensated for by the user. Considering that the user is initially on the target path, i.e., the initial normal deviation is $n_H = 0$, the normal deviation of the user position Δn_H after a step Δs is

$$\Delta n_H = (\sqrt{\Delta s^2 \cdot \Delta \kappa^2 + 1} - 1) \cdot \Delta \kappa^{-1} . \tag{3.16}$$

The increment in the normal deviation Δn increases with the initial normal deviation n. This happens because the instantaneous velocity in the user environment also increases with the normal deviation (cf. (3.9)). Thus, the deviation increment for the user's hand position Δn_E, which is assumed to have an initial deviation from the user path n_E, is

$$\Delta n_E = (\sqrt{\Delta s^2 \cdot \Delta \kappa^2 + 1} - 1) \cdot (\Delta \kappa^{-1} + n_E) , \tag{3.17}$$

and the increment in normal deviation of the user's hand seen by the user is $\Delta n_E - \Delta n_H = (\sqrt{\Delta s^2 \cdot \Delta \kappa^2 + 1} - 1) \cdot n_E$. The perception threshold for arm position stated by Jones and Hunter [60] is $\text{JND}_d \approx 8\%$.

Example 3.5 Deviation of Hand Position from Expected Position

For a step length $\Delta s = 0.5$ m and a nominal deviation from the path $n = 0.5$ m, the user path curvature should be $\Delta \kappa \leq 0.82$ m^{-1}, so that the user does not perceive the normal deviation from the expected hand position.

In addition, when the user interacts with an object in the target environment, small deviations of the user's hand position result in interaction forces that are different from those expected by the user. Consider the following scenario again: The user is walking parallel to a straight wall that he/she is in contact with. For typical values $\Delta \kappa = 0.5$ m^{-1},

$\Delta s = 0.5$ m, and $n = 0.5$ m, the deviation of the user's hand position is $\Delta n_E - \Delta n_H = 0.0154$ m. While rendering, for example, a simple virtual wall, modeled as a spring with stiffness K, the force difference would be $\Delta F = K \cdot 0.0154$ N. Since the JND reported by [26, 131] $\frac{\Delta F}{F} \times 100$ for medium forces perceived by hand and arm is $\mathrm{JND}_f \approx 10\%$, the user would notice the difference when the expected penetration depth into the virtual wall is smaller than 0.154 m, independently of the value of K.

∎

3.5. Summary

In this chapter, the algorithmic framework, which provides haptic naviga-tion assistance in arbitrarily large target environments, has been presented. Assuming that the intended goal (or set of goals) is known, the path predic-tion module infers the desired path toward the goal(s) by assuming either a *path-directed* or a *goal-directed* locomotion model. On the basis of this in-ferred path, the *Plenhaptic Guidance Function* (PHGF) yields the preferred direction of motion and the amount of guidance at each direction.

If the target environment and the user environment had the same size, the wide-are haptic guidance would be accomplished with the rendering of the PHGF with convenient *force control methods*. However, in the case of arbitrarily large target environments, the haptic guidance information (as well as the contact force from the target environment) has to be transformed into the user environment.

For this purpose, the intended *target path* is transformed with Motion Compression into the *user path*, which fits into the user environment. The visual guidance of the user on the user path yields an instantaneous position-dependent transformation between the target and the user envi-ronments. In order to provide the user with consistent visual and haptic information, the haptic information is transformed with the inverse of this transformation, in such a way that the instantaneous mapping of the haptic vectors is a rotation around the vertical axis. The velocity of the rotation of the haptic vectors (and, consequently, the inconsistencies between the expected and the perceived haptic information) depends on the difference of curvature between the target and the user paths and on the current velocity of the user along the user path.

4. The Plenhaptic Guidance Function

The concept of haptic navigation assistance for extended range telepresence is illustrated in Fig. 4.1. As explained in previous chapter, the haptic guidance information is calculated in the target environment and transformed with the corresponding Motion Compression transformation back into the user environment. The transformed haptic guidance information is rendered and superimposed on the transformed recorded haptic information from the target environment. The information is then presented to the user through a suitable haptic interface.

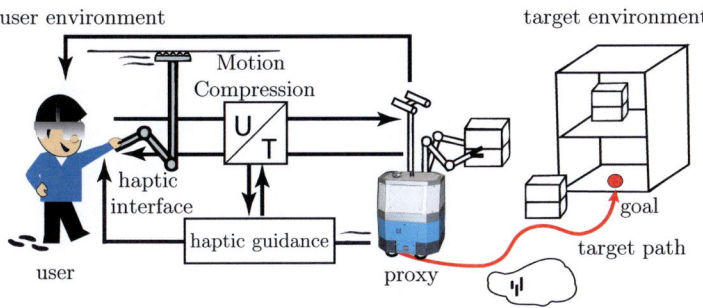

Fig. 4.1.: Concept of wide-area haptic guidance.

This chapter's focus will be on the calculation of the haptic guidance information. While most existing haptic assist functions only provide guidance for simply predefined tasks, we present a guidance function that systematically considers context information, in such a way, that it can easily adapt itself to new user intentions and to the changed geometry of the target environment.

The proposed function provides the guidance information to guide the user on convenient paths or to desired goals, while keeping the proxy away from certain forbidden regions. To achieve natural guidance, the function relies on two human navigation models that result in two types of navigation assistance: *path-directed guidance* and *goal-directed guidance*. Furthermore, the general representation of the guidance information provided by this guidance function allows the guidance information to be used with different types of navigation assistance and haptic rendering methods.

4.1. The Plenhaptic Guidance Function

Given information about the geometry and the points of interest of a scene in the target environment, a guidance function is sought that assists the user in reaching the possible goals but still leaves the operator the control to choose and change his goal. We call this function the *Plenhaptic Guidance Function* (PHGF).

The proposed PHGF defines the intensity of the guidance at any position in space, at any direction, and at any time, and exploits the analogy with the *Plenoptic Function* in vision, which describes the visual information available to an observer at any point in space and time. This analogy is illustrated in Fig. 4.2.

In analogy to vision, a human operator can learn about the objects in the scene by means of active exploration through touch. Therefore, we suggest a *Plenhaptic Function* that formally specifies the amount of haptic stimuli passing through the human's hand and/or the human's fingers for a given position in the space, a given exploration angle, and a given time [144]. The task of the haptic perception is to extract a useful description of the Plenhaptic Function's properties in terms of, for example, experienced forces. The actual information extracted by the human haptic perception system is

Fig. 4.2.: Analogy of the Plenhaptic Guidance Function (PHGF) with the Plenoptic Function.

a small subset of the information that is physically available in the plenhaptic function, since humans gather haptic information from a certain number of positions at a time, obtaining samples from each exploring direction. However, recent work by [49] points out that this function, when it actually exists, is infinite dimensional, and that the number of dimensions needed to specify touch could only be estimated with certain simplified representations of mechanical interactions.

Thus, finding the Plenhaptic Function, or even a simplification of this function, is a very arduous task that goes beyond of the scope of this work. In fact, we are interested in describing the haptic information that is used to guide the user, i.e., a small subset of the whole haptic information available, by means of a function that describes the intensity of the guidance information of a scene at any location of the user $\underline{x}$, at any possible exploring direction defined by the angle α, and at any time t. It takes the general form

$$\text{PHGF} = \text{PHGF}\left(\underline{x}, \alpha, t\right) \ . \tag{4.1}$$

Please note that in the present case, in which the guidance takes place on the horizontal plane, α is 1D. In the case of haptic guidance in 3D-space, α should be 2D. The intensity of the guidance is associated with the *quality* of the directions, since the goal of haptic guidance is to guide the user along *favorable* directions that lead to the goals and to avoid *unfavorable* directions that would lead to collisions with obstacles. Since there are different possibilities of guiding a user, the PHGF is not unique.

In this work, PHGFs for two different human navigation models that result in two types of navigation assistance — *path-directed guidance* and *goal-directed guidance* — were designed. These navigation models are presented in Section 4.2. The first step in the calculation of the PHGFs is to find the most favorable direction of motion in each case, called *guidance direction*, which is the aim of Sections 4.3 and 4.4. The derivation of the PHGFs from the calculated desired directions of motion is presented in Section 4.5.

Normalization of PHGF

From now on, it is assumed that the PHGF is normalized, i.e., returns positive values between *zero* and *one*. The sampled PHGF at a certain position will return *zero* in the direction towards the goal, while the value *one* corresponds to a direction that has to be avoided by all means because it leads to a nearby obstacle or because it leads away from the goal. In the case of being only one possible goal, the PHGF has only one *zero*. However, if several goals can be reached, the PHGF has as many *zeros* as possible goals. Towards other directions the PHGF returns intermediate values.

The normalization function consists of a local offset and a local scaling. First, the normalization function adds an offset, so that the PHGF is always positive and the minimum value of the PHGF at each location is set to *zero*. By doing so, there is always at least one direction at each location in which the user should walk. Second, a scaling factor is used, so that the PHGF is less than or equal to *one* at any location. Fig. 4.3 shows the normalized PHGF at a given position $\underline{x} = (x, y)$ as a function of the orientation defined by α for an exemplary scenario.

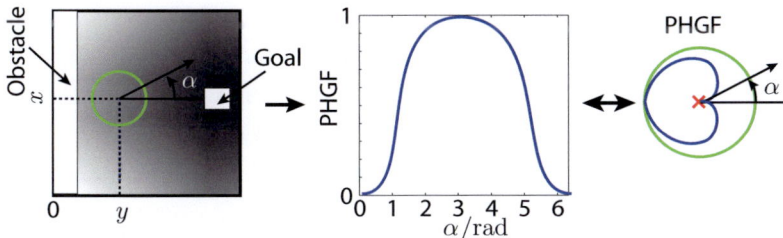

Fig. 4.3.: Normalized PHGF for an exemplary scenario. In the middle picture, the PHGF is plotted for a given position as a function of the orientation. In the right picture, the same function is displayed in polar coordinates (blue line) inside the unit circle (green line).

4.2. Human Navigation Models

Humans possess good navigation capabilities. These capabilities include the ability to build cognitive maps, the ability to make decisions, and the ability to execute decisions [30]. It is an undisputed fact that the visual sense plays a fundamental role in navigation [101]; but so does path integration based on the proprioceptive (or kinesthetic) sense, which is related to the "sense of self-locomotion" provided by neuromuscular spindle, joints, tendons, and forces acting on them [13, 25].

However, while exploring a target environment through a telepresence system, technical limitations imposed to real telepresence systems (e.g., reduced field of view, time-delays, etc.) and certain unfavorable visibility conditions in the target environment (e.g., smoke or darkness) are likely to impair or at least interfere in the execution of the desired navigation task.

For an efficient and intuitive assistance, it is important that the haptic guidance does not demonstrate obtrusive behavior, which would corrupt the feeling of presence, but instead guide the user back to his originally intended actions. Therefore, the guidance assistive function has to take into account human navigation models towards previously selected goals. There are essentially two locomotion models in the literature.

In [81], a locomotion model is presented in which the human orientates himself towards an originally desired path and tries to return to this when he/she leaves it. For this model, the reference point is a point on the path that is, for example, a step forwards on the originally desired path. Such behavior is more realistic when the path is signposted or surrounded by obstacles.

A goal-directed locomotion model instead takes the goal as reference point at each time step and chooses the shortest path to this goal [109]. In the presence of obstacles, the user actualizes his plan at each time step with respect to the goal from his/her current position, by calculating the shortest or quickest path that avoids the obstacles [71].

Based on these two different navigations models, two types of haptic navigation assistance will be presented: *path-directed guidance* and *goal-directed guidance*. With *path-directed guidance*, the desired path is calculated once, as is the path transformation into the user environment. Guiding the user back to the desired target path is equivalent to guiding the user on the calculated user path. By doing this, the geometry of the user environment is also implicitly considered in the haptic guidance.

With *goal-directed guidance*, the optimal path towards the goal is re-calculated from the current user position by considering the presence of obstacles. This calculated path is optimal in the sense of globally minimizing the distance to the desired goal. The calculated path is transformed with Motion Compression into a new feasible user path at each time step in order to provide consistent guidance in the user environment as well. This type of navigation assistance is dynamic, i.e., it can adapt itself to new predicted goals and detected obstacles, since it does not rely on any predefined path, but is calculated dynamically.

Fig. 4.4 illustrates both types of guidance according to the presented human navigation models. In *goal-directed guidance*, the goal position $\underline{x}_g$ is the reference point towards which the user is guided. In this case, $\underline{d}_{r,g}$ designates the desired direction of motion. In contrast, in *path-directed guidance*, the user is controlled so as to return to the originally planned target path and the reference point is an arbitrary point p on the path. In this case, the desired direction of motion is designated by $\underline{d}_{r,p}$.

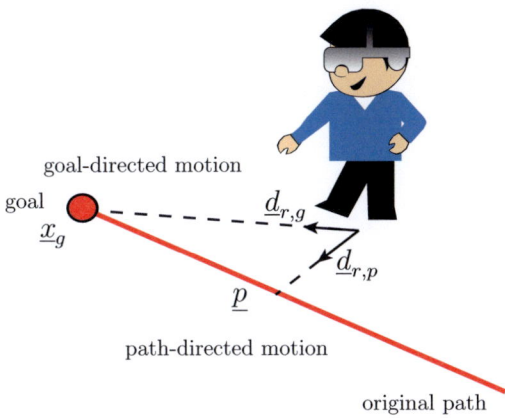

Fig. 4.4.: Human navigation models. In the goal-directed locomotion model, the goal position is the reference point. In the path-directed locomotion model, the user tries to return to the originally planned target path and the reference point is an arbitrary point on the path.

4.3. Path-directed Guidance

Path-directed guidance, as here described, aims at keeping the user on a desired target path. Since deviations occur due to human natural dynamics and cannot be predicted in advance, it is necessary to control the position of the user in order to reduce them. In *path-directed guidance*, the desired direction of motion, or *guidance direction*, depends on the position of the user, the position of the goal, and the desired target path.

The desire is to smoothly guide the user back to the target path in order to avoid oscillations around the path. For this purpose, a *guidance field* is defined that consists of guidance directions that smoothly return the user to the path. The guidance direction at the user position x depends on the nearest point on the desired path x_p, the tangent direction of the path at this point $t(x_p)$, and the orthogonal direction to the path from x, $e(x_p)$. The proposed guidance field assigns a guidance direction $d_{r,p}$ to the current user position x defined as

$$d_{r,p}(x) = \frac{1}{C(x,x_p)} \left(K(x,x_p) t(x_p) + (1 - K(x,x_p)) e(x_p) \right), \qquad (4.2)$$

with

$$K(x,x_p) = \exp\left(\frac{-\|x - x_p\|^{K_2}}{K_1} \right), \qquad (4.3)$$

and the normalization factor $C(x,x_p)$

$$C(x,x_p) = \sqrt{2K(x,x_p)^2 - 2K(x,x_p) + 1} . \qquad (4.4)$$

This guidance field assigns a guidance direction that either points toward the path, in the event that the operator has left it, or points along the path, otherwise. The exponential function ensures a smooth transition between the guidance toward the path due to $e(x_p)$ and the guidance along the path due to $t(x_p)$. Two parameters K_1 and K_2 are used to configure the *path width* and the *curvature* of the guidance field respectively. By defining the *path width* W as the distance from the path at which tangent and orthogonal directions have the same weighting, i.e., $K = 1/2$, the guidance field can easily be configured for $K_2 = 1$ to get a path width W by setting K_1 to

$$K_1 = \frac{W}{\ln(2)} .$$

By increasing K_2, the guidance field converges faster towards the tangent direction inside W and towards the orthogonal direction outside W, i.e., the

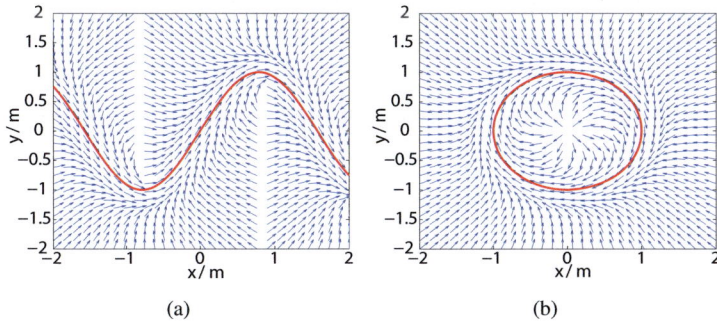

Fig. 4.5.: Guidance fields with parameters $K_1 = 0.5$ and $K_2 = 2$ for two exemplary target paths (red line).

curvature of the guidance field increases. Fig. 4.5 shows the guidance fields for two target paths with $K_1 = 0.5$ and $K_2 = 2$.

Until now, the path-directed guidance has only been spatial, i.e., the guidance direction depends only on the user position. In a temporal approach for path-directed guidance, or *trajectory-directed* guidance, the user has to reach, at each time instant t, a certain point on the path $\underline{p}(t)$. In this case, the time-dependent guidance direction can be calculated as

$$\underline{d}_{r,p}(\underline{x},t) = \frac{\underline{x} - \underline{p}(t)}{\left\| \underline{x} - \underline{p}(t) \right\|} . \tag{4.5}$$

4.4. Goal-directed Guidance

4.4.1. Goal-directed Guidance without Obstacles

In *goal-directed guidance*, the user is assisted in reaching his/her goal. In the absence of obstacles, the user will approach the goal through the shortest path, according to the goal-directed human navigation model. Therefore, the desired target path at each time step is the connecting path from the user to the goal and the instantaneous guidance direction, which points toward the intended goal, is defined by

$$\underline{d}_{r,g}(\underline{x}) = \frac{\underline{x} - \underline{x}_g}{\left\| \underline{x} - \underline{x}_g \right\|} \, , \tag{4.6}$$

where $\underline{x}$ is the position of the user and $\underline{x}_g$ the position of the goal.

Please note that the same expression is used for the calculation of the time-dependent guidance direction. In fact, temporal or trajectory-directed guidance is a special case of goal-directed guidance in the absence of obstacles, in which the position of the intended goal changes at each time step.

4.4.2. Goal-directed Guidance with Obstacles

In the presence of obstacles, the user plans his/her motions in such a way that he/she is able to reach his/her goal without colliding with the obstacles. The same strategy is followed by *goal-directed guidance* so that the guidance direction has to lead the user to the goal by avoiding the obstacles. This problem is referred to as motion planning. Fig. 4.6 shows an exemplary scenario that motivates the need for goal-directed guidance.

A common method for motion planning, particularly suited to online planning problems, is the artificial potential method. With standard artificial potentials, the user moves under the influence of a potential U obtained as the superposition of an attractive potential to the goal and a repulsive potential from the obstacle region. Planning takes place in an incremental fashion: towards the direction defined by the negative gradient $-\nabla U$ of the potential, which indicates the most promising direction of local motion [63,114,126]. However, whatever technique is used to plan motions on the basis of standard artificial potentials, local minima represent a problem.

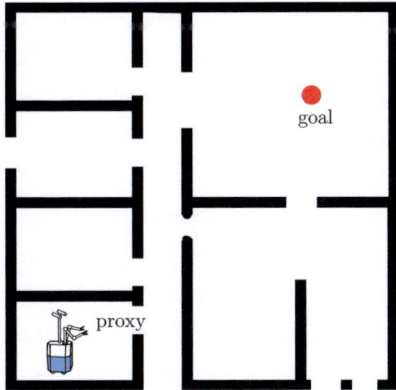

Fig. 4.6.: Exemplary scenario for goal-directed guidance with obstacles.

Navigation Functions

An approach based on *navigation functions*, which are artificial potentials without local minima, is followed in this work to plan the motion toward the goal. *Navigation functions* were first introduced by [102].

A computationally efficient implementation of a navigation function is the *numerical navigation function*. This potential is built on a grid map by assigning the value *zero* to the cell containing the goal and the value *one* to its adjacent cells, the value *two* to the unvisited cells among those adjacent to cells with potential *one*, and so on. The procedure can be visualized as a wavefront that expands according to the *wavefront expansion algorithm*.

Another type of navigation functions that provide an optimal path towards the goal are *harmonic functions*. Harmonic functions (also known as *potential functions* in physics and engineering) are the solution of a particular differential equation, the Laplace or potential equation $\nabla^2 \phi = 0$. In the real world, many physical problems are described by the Laplace equation: velocity field of incompressible fluid, steady-state electric charge distribution, or heat transmission. Harmonic functions can present *stagnation points* in which the velocity of a fluid particle becomes zero instantaneously. However this stagnation point is an unstable saddle point, not a local minimum. Therefore, harmonic functions have received increased interest for obstacle avoidance and path planning of mobile robots [27,28,67].

For *goal-directed guidance*, a harmonic function P is defined over the 2D-domain of interest in the target environment. Since harmonic functions have their maximum and minimum at the boundaries of the closed region defined by the free configuration space [114], *constant Dirichlet's conditions* are applied that assign a constant positive value c to the boundaries of the obstacles and assign the value *zero* to the boundaries of a small region around the goal. This definition implies that the gradient close to obstacles is perpendicular outward from the obstacles' surface.

The guidance direction towards the goal in the presence of obstacles is thus defined by the negative gradient of the harmonic function P as

$$\underline{d}_{r,g}(\underline{x},t) = -\frac{\nabla P(\underline{x},t)}{\|\nabla P(\underline{x},t)\|} \; . \tag{4.7}$$

The desired target path can be calculated by connecting the current user position and the goal position by following the steepest gradient descent of the harmonic function towards the goal. The path produced by this method is optimal in the sense of globally minimizing the distance to the goal as well as locally minimizing a hitting probability [132]. Efficient online calculations of solution paths using harmonic functions are presented in [103, 104].

However, since both the path transformation and the path prediction are dynamic in goal-directed guidance, it is not necessary to transform the whole path, but only the first part of the path beginning at the current user position, the *planning reference point*. Furthermore, since the optimal target path resulting from the harmonic function is smooth (harmonic functions have continuous second order derivatives and thus ∇P is differentiable), a straight target path that begins at the user position and has the direction of $\underline{d}_{r,g}$ can be assumed at each time step. The real-time incremental path transformation presented in [81, 106] (which assumes that the target path is represented as a set of straight segments, and consequently, that the transformed user path is a set of path segments with constant curvature) can then be used. Please note that the geometry of the user environment is implicitly taken into account when transforming the guidance direction into the user environment, since the mapping considers the limits of the user environment.

4.5. Calculation of PHGF

4.5.1. Calculation of PHGF for a Single Goal

So far, the guidance direction for both types of assistance, path-directed and goal-directed guidance, has been calculated. With the former, a desired path is calculated once, and the user is guided back to this path. With the latter, the desired target path and the guidance direction to reach the goal by avoiding the obstacles are calculated online from the current user position. This information is now used to calculate the sought PHGF, first for a single preselected goal i. This function will be called PHGF_i.

The calculation of this function for goal-directed guidance is considered in first place. The harmonic function that considers all the obstacles and one possible goal i, which depends (in the most general case) on the user location $\underline{x}$ and the time t, will be called $P_i(\underline{x}, t)$.

Since the value of the PHGF in each direction represents the quality of this direction with respect to the guidance at a certain position and time, the

57

value of PHGF$_i$ can be calculated by means of the directional derivative D_α of the harmonic function $P_i(\underline{x},t)$, which is defined by

$$D_\alpha(\underline{x},\alpha,t) = \lim_{s \to 0} \frac{P_i(\underline{x}+s\underline{u}(\alpha),t) - P_i(\underline{x},t)}{s} ,$$

as follows

$$\text{PHGF}_i(\underline{x},\alpha,t) = \text{norm}(D_\alpha(\underline{x},\alpha,t)) , \tag{4.8}$$

where $\underline{u}(\alpha)$ is a unit vector in the direction defined by α, and $\text{norm}(\cdot)$ is the normalization function that was explained in Section 4.1.

Since the harmonic function is strictly monotonically decreasing towards the goal location, which is the global minimum of the function, there is at least one direction that leads towards the goal from any user position. This direction, which is the guidance direction, is the only one in which the PHGF$_i$ returns a value of *zero*. In the improbable case in which $\underline{x}$ lies exactly on a stagnation point (D_α would be *zero* in all directions), the increment quotient, instead of the limit in (4.8), has to be used to derive PHGF$_i$.

Recalling the normalization described in Section 4.1, the Plenhaptic Guidance Function for one goal PHGF$_i$ can be obtained by normalizing the directional derivative $D_\alpha(\underline{x},\alpha,t)$ as

$$\text{norm}(D_\alpha(\underline{x},\alpha,t)) = (D_\alpha(\underline{x},\alpha,t) - m(\underline{x},t)) \frac{1}{M(\underline{x},t)} , \tag{4.9}$$

where m is the local offset and M the local scaling, which can be calculated as follows:

$$m(\underline{x},t) = \min_\alpha \{D_\alpha(\underline{x},\alpha,t)\} = -\|\nabla P_i(\underline{x},t)\| , \tag{4.10}$$

and

$$M(\underline{x},t) = \max_{\alpha} \{D_\alpha - m(\underline{x},t)\} = 2\|\nabla P_i(\underline{x},t)\| . \qquad (4.11)$$

On the other hand the directional derivative $D_\alpha(\underline{x},\alpha,t)$ can be expressed as

$$D_\alpha(\underline{x},\alpha,t) = \nabla P_i(\underline{x},t) \cdot \underline{u}(\alpha) ,$$

and from (4.7) and (4.9), PHGF$_i$ can be expressed as

$$\text{PHGF}_i(\underline{x},\alpha,t) = \frac{1}{2}(-\underline{d}_{r,g}(\underline{x},t) \cdot \underline{u}(\alpha) + 1) . \qquad (4.12)$$

The same procedure can be thus generalized for path-directed guidance in order to calculate the function PHGF$_i$, by replacing $\underline{d}_{r,g}$ with $\underline{d}_{r,p}$, i.e., the guidance direction for path-directed guidance. By using this function, the more distant the direction from the guidance direction, the higher the value of the PHGF for this direction, which is in accordance with the definition of PHGF.

From now on, it is assumed that the guidance information is sampled at the current user position. As a result, the PHGF at the sampled position and time is a scalar function that depends only on direction. The PHGF is then sampled for sufficient directions and transformed with Motion Compression back into the user environment, where it can be rendered by different *force control methods* presented in Section 5.3. Since the PHGF is normalized, the final strength of the haptic commands can be scaled depending on the rendering method, the haptic device, the current user performance, etc. Moreover, by using a normalized PHGF, it is possible to generalize the function in order to guide the user to multiple goals.

4.5.2. Calculation of PHGF for Several Goals

In the previous subsection, the Plenhaptic Guidance Function PHGF_i for one goal i has been obtained. However, in a large target environment several goals may be equally probable. These goals are called *simultaneous*, in which case the haptic guidance has to permit the user to decide which goal he/she wants to walk to, i.e., simultaneous goals have to be equally reachable with the PHGF.

In order to allow the user to reach simultaneous goals, and assuming the resulting PHGF is *zero* along the possible guidance directions, the functions PHGF_i for each goal have to be combined with a certain *t-norm* [68]. The combination of the functions PHGF_i with a t-norm makes it possible to walk to simultaneous goals because the *zeros* of the PHGF_i are preserved in the resulting PHGF at the same locations. Furthermore, since the PHGF_i are derived from harmonic functions that consider the same obstacles, all PHGF_i will have high values (close to *one*) in the directions towards the obstacles (due to the *constant Dirichlet's conditions*), and the information of the resulting PHGF will be consistent. The PHGF is obtained as follows:

$$\text{PHGF}(\underline{x}, \alpha, t) = \overset{G}{\underset{i=1}{T}} \{\text{PHGF}_i(\underline{x}, \alpha, t)\} , \qquad (4.13)$$

where G is the number of simultaneous goals.

The most common t-norm is the *minimum t-norm*. By combining the functions PHGF_i for each goal with the *minimum t-norm*, the resulting PHGF allows the user to choose among all potential goal locations. Since the minimum t-norm is the largest t-norm [68], by using another t-norm the level of guidance towards the non-preferred directions will tend to be lower. Fig. 4.7 illustrates the concept of PHGF for the different types of guidance.

Please note that the choice between simultaneous goals is only possible because individual PHGF_i for each goal were used. If the resulting PHGF had been derived from only one harmonic function that considered all possible goal locations, the goals would be *exclusive*, in the sense that the PHGF would guide the user only to one of the goal locations, namely to the closest one.

Although the rendering of the PHGF leaves as many goal alternatives open as possible at the current position, Motion Compression has to choose one of the goals and the corresponding target path for calculating the new transformation, at the latest when the user has started motion towards one of these simultaneous goals. In the case of path-directed guidance, the user could choose between several paths. In this case, the transformation would not be static anymore, since Motion Compression would have to change the path transformation for each of the alternative paths in order to provide consistent guidance.

A time-variant PHGF is necessary when dealing with moving obstacles or dynamic scenes. As the harmonic function has to be calculated globally, its calculation is largely dependent on the area of the scene A. Due to the necessity to calculate the $PHGF_i$ for all goals G, the resulting complexity for the potential function calculation becomes $\mathcal{O}(AG)$. The derivative calculation for all discrete directions N at the current point $\underline{x}$ adds the further, but usually negligible, complexity of $\mathcal{O}(N)$. In the case that the number of goals increases drastically, the computation time can be reduced by reducing the spatial resolution of the PHGF.

4.6. Summary

The PHGF provides the necessary guidance information both for guiding the user towards targets and target paths and for avoiding obstacles by considering, systematically and in real time, context information from the target environment. The center of the functions, as well as the center of Motion Compression, is the user position, although the user is then guided by means of haptic commands applied on the user's hand.

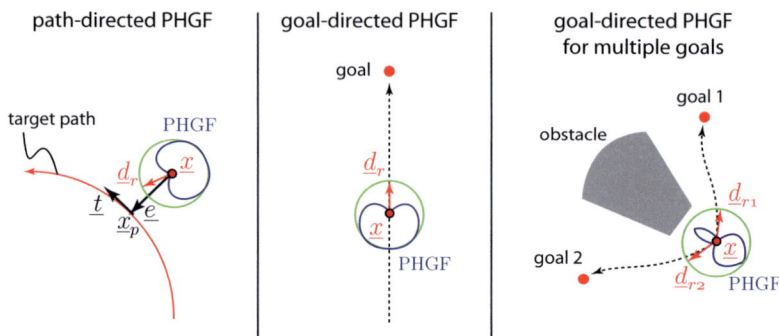

Fig. 4.7.: PHGFs for different types of haptic guidance. In path-directed guidance
(left), the user motion is controlled so as to be along a certain path. In
goal-directed guidance (middle), the user is guided toward a specific target. In goal-directed guidance with obstacles (right), the user is kept away
from obstacle regions. When goal-directed guidance for multiple simultaneous goals is used (right), the user can choose which target he/she wants
to walk to.

Two types of navigation assistance that are based on the typical human
navigation models have been presented: *path-directed guidance* and *goal-
directed guidance*. The switching between the models depends on the task
in the target environment. While path-directed guidance steers the user toward a reference path, goal-directed guidance recalculates the optimal path
towards the goal from the current user position by considering the presence
of obstacles. By using this method, it is possible to adapt the guidance
function to new predicted goals and obstacles, since it does not rely on predefined paths, but instead dynamically calculates and transforms the path
with Motion Compression. In any case, the limits of the user environment
are implicitly considered in the guidance by means of the path transformation.

If several equally probable goals, or *simultaneous goals*, exist, the PHGF
leaves every possibility open for as long as possible. This is particularly
useful when the intention recognition fails, or when it cannot distinguish

between several goals. The new transformation is then calculated once the user has moved towards one of those targets.

The final strength of the haptic guidance commands is calculated by rendering the PHGF with adequate *force control methods*. The force control methods transform the guidance information into intuitive haptic cues in which the level, i.e., the strength, of the guidance can be adjusted so that the user can always overcome the guidance, as will be explained in the next chapter.

5. Haptic Guidance of User

The haptic guidance information provided by the PHGF is transformed into haptic commands that are superimposed to the haptic information from the application and applied on the user's hand. This process is called rendering of the PHGF.

In the rendering process, two important challenges have to be faced. On the one hand, control laws have to be found in order to control the position and the orientation of the user by means of forces applied on his/her hand, which is equivalent to controlling an *underactuated* system. On the other hand, since the user has to preserve the control over the task, as well as the feeling of presence in the target environment, a trade-off between performance and transparency, or, equivalently, between motion restriction and motion freedom, has to be achieved.

In this chapter we present two *force control methods* to render the PHGF, methods that effectively guide the user towards the desired directions. *Active force control* performs the guidance by means of guidance forces. On the contrary, with *passive force control*, a direction-dependent guidance is performed by favoring the motion towards the desired directions and restricting the motion in the other directions.

In order to identify the influence of the level of guidance on user performance, a user study has been conducted, and those results are presented in Section 5.4. The previous user study presented in [146] was extended here in order to evaluate not only active and passive force control methods, but also the combination of both. Furthermore, gathered experimental data has been used to approximate static relationships between performance measures and assistance level, which allows us to predict user performance and adjust the assistance level depending on the requirements of the task.

5.1. User Model

In order to find adequate force control methods that effectively guide the user towards the desired direction, a kinematic and dynamic model of the user has to be considered. The user walking in the extended range telepresence system usually walks tangentially to the user path and rarely walks sidewards or backwards. On the other hand, the user is guided by means of planar forces, which are applied to his/her hand. Under the assumption that the user holds his/her hand in front of his/her body while walking, the dynamics of the user can be modeled as a wheeled mobile robot with a nonholonomic constraint (which formally cancels sidewards motion), in which the inputs are Cartesian forces applied on the user's hand instead of torques τ_1 and τ_2 on the wheels. Fig. 5.1 illustrates this analogy.

The user configuration is then completely described by $\underline{x} = [x, y, \theta]^T$, where $[x, y]$ are the Cartesian coordinates of the body and θ is the orientation of the body with respect to the x axis. The kinematic model of the user can be then expressed as

$$\begin{bmatrix} \dot{x} \\ \dot{y} \\ \dot{\theta} \end{bmatrix} = \begin{bmatrix} \cos\theta \\ \sin\theta \\ 0 \end{bmatrix} v + \begin{bmatrix} 0 \\ 0 \\ 1 \end{bmatrix} w , \tag{5.1}$$

where the inputs are the driving velocity v, which is the magnitude, with sign, of the user's velocity vector, and the steering velocity w, which is the angular speed around the vertical axis. Such a system is called *underactuated* because there are less inputs than states. Since nonholonomic underactuated systems are not linearly controllable [10], but satisfy *small-time local controllability* [115], they have to be controlled using time-varying and/or discontinuous feedback controllers [114].

The corresponding dynamic model of the user, which is equivalent to the dynamic model of the wheeled robot, can be represented using the driving force F_u and the steering torque $\tau = LF_v$ as inputs. Let m be the mass of the user and I be the moment of inertia around the vertical axis. The dynamic model incorporates two new states $\dot{v}$ and $\dot{w}$, which satisfy

$$\begin{bmatrix} \dot{v} \\ \dot{w} \end{bmatrix} = \begin{bmatrix} \frac{1}{m} F_u \\ \frac{1}{I} LF_v \end{bmatrix} . \tag{5.2}$$

The analogy with the wheeled robot is straightened by expressing the velocity inputs as a function of the angular speeds of the wheels of the robot (w_1 and w_2) as

$$\begin{bmatrix} v \\ w \end{bmatrix} = \begin{bmatrix} \frac{R}{2}(w_1 + w_2) \\ \frac{R}{2a}(w_2 - w_1) \end{bmatrix} , \tag{5.3}$$

and the force inputs as a function of the wheel torques of the robot (τ_1 and τ_2) as

$$\begin{bmatrix} F_u \\ LF_v \end{bmatrix} = \begin{bmatrix} \frac{1}{R}(\tau_1 + \tau_2) \\ \frac{a}{R}(\tau_2 - \tau_1) \end{bmatrix} . \tag{5.4}$$

5.2. Motion Control of User

In the previous chapter, the problem of motion planning was addressed and the desired direction of motion, or guidance direction, was calculated for two typical motion tasks. The problem that arises now is: How is it possible to guide the user on the desired paths or towards the desired directions? Generally, when controlling underactuated systems, there are two basic control problems [114]:

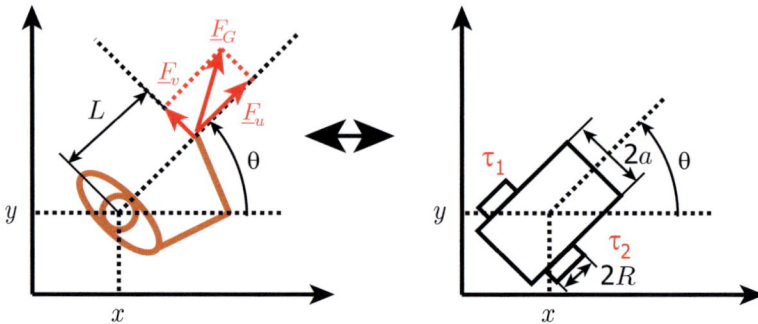

Fig. 5.1.: User modeled as a car-like wheeled mobile robot moving on a plane.

- *Posture regulation*: The user must reach a final posture from an initial configuration. This problem arises when the user is near his/her desired goal, or in an initialization phase, e.g., in which the user has to be steered towards a convenient orientation to start following the desired path.

- *Tracking control*: The user tracks the desired Cartesian path or trajectory starting from an initial configuration that may or may not be on the path. This problem arises when the user moves on a persistent trajectory, i.e., while he/she is guided either with path-directed or with goal-directed guidance.

From a practical point of view, the most relevant of these problems for navigation assistance is certainly the second one. When *posture regulation* is performed, the Cartesian path along which the user approaches the goal cannot be specified in advance. In contrast, with *tracking control*, the user would move along (or close to) the desired direction planned with the PHGF. Furthermore, the human operator can easily decide, depending on the context, which orientation is the most adequate one for approaching the goal.

The motion problem of underactuated systems is generally formulated with reference to the kinematic model, i.e., by assuming that the control inputs directly determine the generalized velocities. This can be done because in such system it is possible to cancel the dynamic effects via state feedback.

5.2.1. Posture Regulation

The problem of posture regulation consists in designing a feedback control law that drives the user to a desired configuration x_d. Posture regulation is necessary, when the user needs to accurately reach the desired position with a desired orientation. In this case, *tracking control* can be performed until the user comes in close proximity to the goal, whereupon *posture regulation* is performed.

Due to the nonholonomic constraint, the system does not admit any *universal* controller. Therefore, the posture regulation must be addressed using purposely designed control laws. As a matter of fact, it can be proven that any feedback law that can regulate the posture of this underactuated system must necessarily be discontinuous with respect to the state and/or time-varying [10, 114]. Without loss of generality, it can be assumed that the desired configuration is the origin.

First, only the case of Cartesian regulation is considered. The Cartesian error is then simply $[-x, -y]$. With reference to Fig. 5.2, let us define the polar coordinates such that

$$
\begin{aligned}
\rho &= \sqrt{x^2 + y^2}\,, \\
\gamma &= \text{Atan2}(y, x) - \theta + \pi\,, \\
\delta &= \gamma + \theta\,.
\end{aligned}
\tag{5.5}
$$

It can be proven (see [114] for more details) that the Cartesian error asymptotically converges to zero by using the following control law

$$
\begin{aligned}
v &= k_1 \rho \cos \gamma, \\
w &= k_2 \gamma.
\end{aligned}
\tag{5.6}
$$

where $k_1 > 0, k_2 > 0$. These commands have an immediate geometric interpretation: The driving velocity v is proportional to the projection of the Cartesian error on the sagittal axis (the heading direction) of the user, whereas the steering velocity w is proportional to the difference between the orientation of the user and that of the Cartesian error vector $\underline{e}_p = \underline{x}_d - \underline{x}$ (c.f. Fig. 5.2).

In order to control the final orientation as well, another controller is required. In [114], the following feedback control law is defined for this purpose

$$
\begin{aligned}
v &= k_1 \rho \cos \gamma, \\
w &= k_2 \gamma + k_1 \frac{\sin \gamma \cos \gamma}{\gamma} (\gamma + k_3 \delta).
\end{aligned}
\tag{5.7}
$$

The driving velocity coincides with that of (5.6) but the steering velocity differs from that of (5.6) in that there is a second term that implicitly considers the orientation error θ (which is included in the variable δ).

Since the user is controlled by forces applied on his hand, the input in the form of Cartesian forces applied on the user's hand are related to the input velocities by

$$
\underline{F}_G =
\begin{bmatrix}
\cos \theta & -\sin \theta \\
\sin \theta & \cos \theta
\end{bmatrix}
\begin{bmatrix}
1/m & 0 \\
0 & L/I
\end{bmatrix}
\begin{bmatrix}
\dot{v} \\
\dot{w}
\end{bmatrix}.
\tag{5.8}
$$

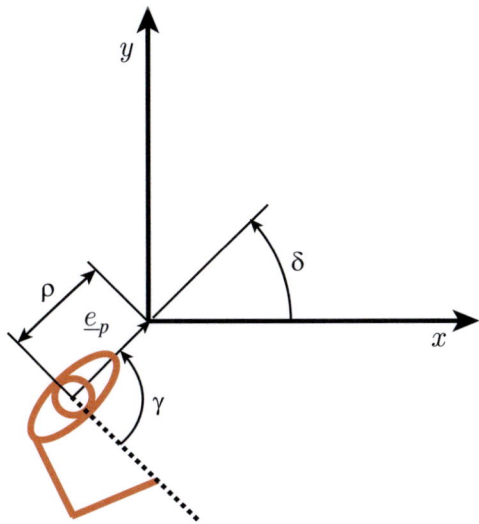

Fig. 5.2.: Posture regulation problem for an underactuated system.

5.2.2. Tracking Control

The previous approach is not adequate for path tracking since the covered path cannot be controlled, but only the final position, so that *posture regulation* should only be used to initialize the guidance or when the user has almost reached the target and there is no obstacle near the target. However, for wide-area haptic guidance, in which the user is guided along certain paths or desired directions, the *tracking control* problem has to be solved. The general problem of tracking a desired trajectory is nonlinear and time-varying. Furthermore, it is necessary that the desired Cartesian trajectory given by $\underline{x}_d(t) = [x_d(t), y_d(t), \theta_d(t)]^T$ be admissible for the kinematic model. Fig. 5.3 illustrates the tracking control problem. However, while the user is tracking a path, the exact orientation during the motion is usually not relevant. Therefore, only the Cartesian error $\underline{e}_p = \underline{x}_d - \underline{x}$ will be considered. In our system, the choice of $\underline{x}_d(t)$ depends on the type of assistance.

In *temporal path-directed* (or *trajectory-directed*) guidance, the desired configuration at any time $\underline{x}_d(t)$, i.e., the trajectory, is known, as illustrated in Fig. 5.3. In contrast, for *spatial guidance* (either path-directed or goal-directed), since there is no time law but a given guidance direction to be followed, $\underline{x}_d(t)$ is chosen so that, from the current configuration $\underline{x}(t)$, $\underline{x}_d(t)$ is situated at a typical step length Δs along the guidance direction $\underline{d}_r(\underline{x},t)$ such that

$$\underline{x}_d(t) = \underline{x}(t) + \Delta s \cdot \underline{d}_r(\underline{x},t) . \tag{5.9}$$

A well-known approach for the tracking control of underactuated systems is based on input/output linearization via feedback [114]. This approach makes use of the fact that the underactuated system can be controlled on arbitrary paths by controlling a point situated at the sagittal axis at a nonzero distance from the user (or the contact points of the wheels in the case of a wheeled robot). Let us consider the following outputs

$$
\begin{aligned}
x_E &= x + L\cos\theta , \\
y_E &= y + L\sin\theta ,
\end{aligned}
\tag{5.10}
$$

with $L > 0$. The dependency on t is removed in the following for simplicity. x_E and y_E represent the Cartesian coordinates of a point E located along the sagittal axis of the user at a distance L ahead of the user. The time derivatives of x_E and y_E are

$$
\begin{bmatrix} \dot{x}_E \\ \dot{y}_E \end{bmatrix} = \begin{bmatrix} \cos\theta & -L\sin\theta \\ \sin\theta & L\cos\theta \end{bmatrix} \begin{bmatrix} v \\ w \end{bmatrix} = \mathbf{T}(\theta) \begin{bmatrix} v \\ w \end{bmatrix} .
\tag{5.11}
$$

It is now sufficient to use the following input transformation (the matrix **T** is invertible with determinant L)

$$\begin{bmatrix} \dot{v} \\ \dot{w} \end{bmatrix} = \mathbf{T}^{-1}(\theta) \begin{bmatrix} u_x \\ u_y \end{bmatrix} ,$$

to put the equations of user motion in the form

$$\begin{aligned} \dot{x}_E &= u_x , \\ \dot{y}_E &= u_y , \\ \dot{\theta} &= \tfrac{1}{L}(u_y \cos\theta - u_x \sin\theta) . \end{aligned} \qquad (5.12)$$

An input/output linearization via feedback has been obtained. At this point a simple linear controller of the form

$$\begin{aligned} u_x &= \dot{x}_{E,d} + k_x (x_{E,d} - x_E) , \\ u_y &= \dot{y}_{E,d} + k_y (y_{E,d} - y_E) , \end{aligned} \qquad (5.13)$$

with $k_x > 0$, $k_y > 0$, guarantees exponential convergence to a zero Cartesian tracking error, with decoupled dynamics on its two components.

By using this result of the input/output linearization [114], it is possible to make the user track an arbitrary trajectory (the Cartesian tracking error converges to zero) while making a point E, situated ahead of the user, for example the user's hand, track the trajectory

$$\begin{aligned} x_{E,d} &= x_d + L\cos\theta , \\ y_{E,d} &= y_d + L\sin\theta . \end{aligned} \qquad (5.14)$$

The user actually moves on a *smoothed* trajectory compared to the arbitrary desired trajectory followed by the user's hand. This is important, because no assumptions of admissible trajectories have to be made for x_d. This is true as long $L \neq 0$. The orientation of the user under this control is governed by equation (5.12), and is thus not directly controlled.

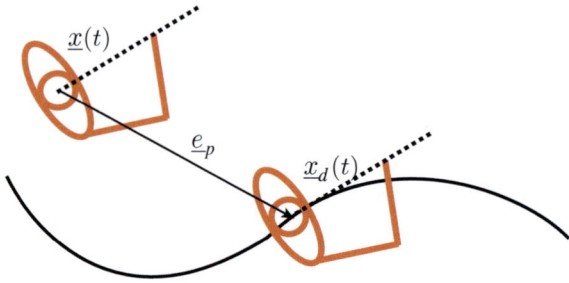

Fig. 5.3.: Tracking control problem for an underactuated system.

Under haptic guidance, the velocity commands cannot be directly applied to the user. Instead, guidance forces calculated via state feedback are applied on the user's hand in order to compensate for deviations from the commanded velocity given by $[u_x, u_y]$

$$
\begin{aligned}
F_x &= k'_x \left(u_x - v_{x,E} \right), \\
F_y &= k'_y \left(u_y - v_{y,E} \right),
\end{aligned}
\tag{5.15}
$$

where $k'_x > 0$, $k'_y > 0$, and $[v_{x,E}, v_{y,E}]$ is the current velocity of the point E. On the other hand, since the user does not follow any desired velocity profile along the path, $[\dot{x}_{E,d}, \dot{y}_{E,d}]$ corresponds to the current velocity, and from (5.13) the state feedback becomes

$$
\begin{aligned}
F_x &= k'_x k_x \left(x_{E,d} - x_E \right), \\
F_y &= k'_y k_y \left(y_{E,d} - y_E \right),
\end{aligned}
\tag{5.16}
$$

or accordingly (5.14)

$$
\begin{aligned}
F_x &= k'_x k_x \left(x_d - x \right), \\
F_y &= k'_y k_y \left(y_d - y \right).
\end{aligned}
\tag{5.17}
$$

Finally, the guidance force $\underline{F}_G$ can be expressed in terms of the guidance direction $\underline{d}_r$ as

$$\underline{F}_G = K \left\| \underline{e}_p \right\| \underline{d}_r \, , \tag{5.18}$$

where $K = \mathrm{diag}(k'_x k_x, k'_y k_y)$ is an arbitrary diagonal positive-definite matrix, and particularly, for path-directed and goal-directed guidance, using (5.9), the guidance force is given by

$$\underline{F}_G = K \, \Delta s \, \underline{d}_r \, . \tag{5.19}$$

As a result, in *spatial path-directed* and *goal-directed* guidance, the user can be guided towards the desired direction of motion by means of a constant guidance force $\underline{F}_G$ towards the guidance direction $\underline{d}_r$. In contrast, when the *temporal* guidance is performed, the magnitude of the guidance force increases with the magnitude of the Cartesian error from the desired Cartesian trajectory.

5.3. Force Control Methods

In the previous section, the guidance forces that are applied to the user's hand to guide the user towards the desired goal or path were calculated. When the exact orientation of the user during the tracking phase is not required, the control input depends only on the Cartesian error from the desired position and on the *guidance direction*, which is calculated according to the navigation methods presented in Chapter 4.

For *spatial guidance*, i.e., when the desired position is not bounded to a time law, the guidance force only depends on the preferred direction of motion. In this case, the user could be guided towards this desired direction not only by actively influencing his/her motion by means of guidance forces, but also by favoring the motion of the user towards the preferred direction, or equivalently, by restricting his/her motion towards the other directions.

This alternative method for spatial guidance will be called the *passive* force control method, in opposition to the *active* force control method, which uses guiding forces. The terms *active* and *passive* make reference to role of the guidance system regarding the motion of the end-effector, to which the user is attached during telepresence operations. Whereas with active force control, the guidance system applies the guidance force, with passive force control, the source of the end-effector motion is the force applied by the user. The benefit of the passive force control method is that the guidance is less intrusive and that the level of motion guidance, i.e., the restriction towards the other directions, can be adjusted using the information provided by the PHGF. In addition, passive and active force control methods can be combined.

These force control methods can be regarded as two different ways of rendering the guidance information provided by the PHGF. At each time step, the PHGF is sampled at the current user position in a finite number of directions, among which the *guidance direction* (at which the PHGF is *zero*) is included. In the case of active force control, the PHGF along the guidance direction is rendered as an active force. In the case of passive force control, the sampled values of the PHGF are rendered as an anisotropic admittance. In both cases, the sampled directions are first mapped into the user environment with the transformation provided by Motion Compression. In the following subsections, further details about these methods are presented.

5.3.1. Active Force Control

When using active guidance to render the PHGF, the user is guided towards his/her goal by means of a guidance force $\underline{F}_G$ that pulls him/her towards the desired direction, which takes the general form

$$\underline{F}_G = \underline{F}_G(\underline{x}, \alpha, t) \ . \tag{5.20}$$

Because the guidance force at each instant t is directed towards the desired direction, the only possibility to guide a user towards a goal with active guidance is to render the PHGF as a certain positive guidance force only along the direction α in which the PHGF has a *zero* value and *zero* guidance force in the other directions.

However, when several simultaneous goals exist, i.e., the PHGF has zero values at several directions, a rendering is required that still allows the user to choose among these goals. One possibility of doing this is to detect which of these goal directions the user is walking to, e.g., by measuring the applied force, and to assist motion in this direction with a positive guidance force. Whereas the user does not take any direction, a *dithering* method can be applied that signalizes which directions lead to possible goals.

For *spatial* goal-directed and path-directed guidance, as explained in previous section, a constant force towards the desired direction is enough to guide the user on the corresponding target path. To maintain a high degree of immersion, the magnitude of the guidance force has to be kept as small as possible while achieving acceptable performance during the navigation. It is only for spatial guidance that the user can be guided by using the alternative passive method, in which the user controls the amount of force in the desired direction. However, for *temporal* guidance, where the magnitude of the guidance force increases with the Cartesian position error from the desired trajectory, or for *pose regulation*, only the active method is able to drive the user towards the desired position. In any case, the guidance force

is transformed into the user environment, added to the transformed interaction force from the target environment, and displayed to the user on the
haptic device.

5.3.2. Passive Force Control

With active guidance, the end-effector may move without an input force
from the user, and this property is often considered undesirable [96]. In
contrast to active force control, with passive force control the commanded
velocity of the manipulator $\dot{x}_{ref}$ is proportional to the force applied by the
user so that the manipulator does not move if the user does not apply any
force. Similar virtual fixtures are presented in [19] for a system for cooperative manipulation.

The passive rendering of the PHGF allows the display of continuous
guidance information in all directions since the user is guided by variably
attenuating the motion in the different directions. The velocity of the manipulator can be written in the absence of a contact force from the target
environment as

$$\underline{\dot{x}}_{E,ref}\,(\underline{x},\,\alpha,\,t) = C\,(\underline{x},\,\alpha,\,t)\,\underline{F}_{meas}\,, \tag{5.21}$$

where $\underline{\dot{x}}_{E,ref}$ is the commanded velocity of the manipulator, $\underline{F}_{meas}$ is the
force applied by the user, and $C(\underline{x},\alpha,t)$ is the anisotropic admittance function that attenuates the motion of the end-effector depending on the direc-
tion α of the applied force at the user location $\underline{x}$ and instant t. Here, α
accounts for the transformed direction in the user environment.

The admittance function $C(\underline{x},\alpha,t)$ relates directions in the user environment to scalar admittance values. To build this admittance function, the
PHGF is first densely sampled, and then the sampled values are transferred
to the respective transformed directions in the user environment (the value
of the function between samples is obtained through interpolation), and
finally the "transformed" PHGF is scaled with a certain scaling function.

The passive rendering of the PHGF simulates a set of virtual damper elements in all directions at the given position, so that when the user moves, for example towards an obstacle, his motion is highly damped, whereas the motions towards possible goals are lowly damped. The value of the damping (the inverse of the admittance value) at each direction is obtained by mapping the values of the transformed PHGF between the minimum and the maximum damping with a monotonically increasing scaling function $S(\cdot)$, such that

$$
\begin{aligned}
D_{min} &= S\left(\text{PHGF}(\underline{x}, \alpha, t)\right) : \text{PHGF}(\underline{x}, \alpha, t) = 0 \,, \\
D_{max} &= S\left(\text{PHGF}(\underline{x}, \alpha, t)\right) : \text{PHGF}(\underline{x}, \alpha, t) = 1 \,.
\end{aligned}
\tag{5.22}
$$

Please note that the lowest displayable damping D_{min} is limited by the stability of the haptic interface. Varying the maximum damping D_{max} creates different levels of guidance, from *very hard* guidance when $D_{min}/D_{max} \rightarrow 0$ to *no guidance* when $D_{min}/D_{max} = 1$, in which case the admittance is isotropic and no guidance occurs. In the intermediate case of *soft* guidance, when $0 << D_{min}/D_{max} < 1$, some motion of the user towards non-preferred directions is allowed. On the contrary, *very hard* guidance leaves the user no or very little freedom to deviate from the preferred direction. A *very hard* guidance is necessary in order to keep the user from entering *forbidden regions* in the target environment [77].

The passive force control method is particularly useful for guiding the user towards multiple *simultaneous* goals since this rendering method leaves every possibility open for the user by displaying no resistance towards the simultaneous goals. For this reason, no decision has to be made by the system in advance. However, the passive rendering method does not allow *trajectory-directed* guidance, since there is any external force to accelerate the user in case the Cartesian error grows bigger with time. The guidance is still time-dependent since the guidance direction at a certain position changes with time, e.g., if a new obstacle appears.

Since the passive rendering method controls the desired velocity of the end-effector, the use of passive guidance with an admittance-controlled haptic display is straightforward. However, haptic guidance with passive force control can also be implemented on an impedance-type device using the so-called *pseudo-admittance framework* [2].

An important benefit of these force control methods is that both active and passive methods can be combined. In this case, the control law of the haptic display becomes

$$\underline{\dot{x}}_{E,ref}\left(\underline{x},\,\alpha,\,t\right) = C\left(\underline{x},\,\alpha,\,t\right)\left(\underline{F}_{meas} - \underline{F}_{ref}\right) \quad, \tag{5.23}$$

where $\underline{F}_{ref}$ is the resultant force presented to the user, which is given by

$$\underline{F}_{ref} = \underline{F}_G + \underline{F}_T \quad, \tag{5.24}$$

where $\underline{F}_G$ is the active guidance force and $\underline{F}_T$ is the contact force from the target environment. Here, the passive force control works as a *virtual coupling* [7] that connects the impedance virtual environment with the admittance-controlled haptic display. As a result, the amount of active and passive guidance can be arbitrarily adjusted.

5.3.3. Adaptation of Level of Guidance

The adaptation of the level of guidance is a challenging issue in every haptic guidance approach because a trade-off between task performance (in terms of execution time and accuracy) and the user's motion freedom is necessary. Generally, an increase in the level of guidance brings an increase in user performance, but usually at the expense of increasing the restriction of the user's motion. Therefore, a measure of the user's motion restriction, e.g., the applied force or the user's effort, has to be taken into account in order to choose the adequate level of guidance. On the other hand, it is crucial that the user can overcome the guidance commands to be able to react to unforeseen events that have not been considered in the haptic assistance.

The first step in order to optimally tune the level of guidance consists in identifying static relationships between the level of guidance and previously defined performance measures experimentally, as proposed in [78]. Then, the level of guidance that maximizes the performance measures on the basis of the identified relationships has to be found. However, as mentioned before, these measures usually deliver conflicting results, so that a trade-off has to be achieved. One solution to this problem is to build a combined performance criterion [87], which considers all performance measures. By optimizing this criterion, the sought trade-off, e.g., between task performance and user effort, can be found.

5.4. Experimental Evaluation of Force Control Methods

5.4.1. Method

The PHGF defines the preferred direction of motion and describes the quality of the other directions with regard to the task of leading the user towards the goal positions, which is directly related to the required amount of guidance. It is the rendering of the PHGF using the presented force control methods that transforms the guidance information into effective haptic commands. The scaling of the PHGF, i.e., the relation between the magnitude of the haptic guidance commands in the "preferred" direction and in the "worst" direction determines the level of guidance, so that when the magnitude of the haptic guidance commands is the same in all directions, no guidance exists.

Real experiments have been performed in order to analyze user performance under the different force control methods and different levels of guidance. The experiments were performed for two typical navigation tasks that require goal-directed and path-directed guidance. The objectives of the test study were: first, to quantify the performance of the user under different guidance conditions; and second, to find the most adequate force control method and level of guidance for each navigation task.

Scenario

Two typical navigation tasks, which represent both navigation methods, were selected. In order to reduce the amount of trials, both tasks were integrated in a combined task consisting of, first, the targeting subtask without obstacles (representing goal-directed guidance) and, second, the path-following subtask (representing path-directed guidance).

The targeting subtask consists of finding two targets placed at random positions in such a way that the total distance between the second target and the start position of the user (via the first target) is the same, 5 m, in all test runs. In this way, the test person cannot learn the location of the target, but the trials can still be compared.

The path-following subtask consists in following a sinus-shaped path. The start position of the path is the last position of the user in the previous subtask (i.e., the position of the second target), and the end-position of the path is again randomly chosen so that the length of the path is the same, 5 m, in all test runs. Fig. 5.4 shows one realization of the combined task together with one exemplary user path during the task.

Performance Measures

Haptic guidance aims to achieve an optimal task performance even while the user still maintains the feeling of presence in the remote environment and the control over the task. Task performance is measured in terms of *execution time*, and in terms of average *error* from the target positions in the case of the targeting task, or average *deviation* from the reference path in the case of the path-following task.

The mean of the applied force is a measure of the *effort* employed by the user to perform the task, and this should be kept as small as possible in order to provide the user with pleasant guidance.

A questionnaire was also used to evaluate the subjective performance of the guidance methods. The subjects were asked which kind of guidance (*active, passive*, or *combined*) they liked most, and which level of guidance (*soft, medium, hard*, or *very hard*) was more adequate for the task in each case.

Guidance Implementation

Experiments were conducted by using the semi-mobile haptic interface, which is described in detail in Chapters 6 and 7.

Active haptic guidance (A) was implemented as a constant guidance force along the guidance direction, $F_G = k$. Four parameters were tested, from *soft* guidance to *very hard* guidance ($k = 8, 10, 13$, and 15 N), which correspond to assistance levels 1, 2, 3, and 4, respectively.

Passive haptic guidance (P) was implemented as a large damping in the "worst" direction $D_\perp$, i.e., the opposite direction to the guidance direction. A small damping along the guidance direction $D_\parallel = 10$ Ns/m is required to ensure the stability of the admittance control. Again, four damping coefficients, $D_\perp$, were tested from *soft* guidance to *very hard* guidance ($D_\perp = 75$, 100, 200, and 400 Ns/m), which correspond to levels of guidance 1, 2, 3, and 4, respectively.

Combined haptic guidance (C) was implemented as a constant active force along the guidance direction, $F_G = 8$ N combined with passive damping in the other directions with increasing parameters ($D_\perp = 75$, 100, 200, and 400 Ns/m) for assistance levels 1, 2, 3, and 4, respectively.

Experimental Design and Participants

In order to investigate the effects of the guidance level and the force control method on task performance and human effort, the amount of guidance was varied on four levels. These variations will be denoted as assistance levels (AL 1-4.) The four assistance levels and the three force control methods (FC A, FC P, FC C) are addressed by a two factorial repeated-measurements experiment design.

A total of eight participants, two women and six men, aging from 22 to 31, one left-handed and seven right-handed, were involved in the experiment. Before data was collected, subjects familiarized themselves with the haptic interface, the task, and the guidance methods.

Participants were instructed to perform the task as quickly and as accurately as possible. The participant performed the task three times in a row with each assistance level. The first trial represented a training trial, while the second and the third trials were used for the analysis. Participants were informed about the total number of assistance levels and they were told when subtask and assistance level changed. The order in which the assistance levels were presented was systematically varied.

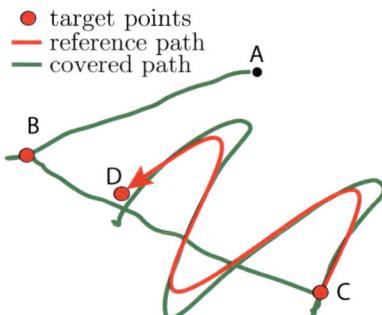

Fig. 5.4.: Combined task used for the guidance experiments, which consists of a targeting subtask (ABC) and a path-following subtask (CD).

5.4.2. Results and Discussion

Normality assumption was checked on all dependent variables to ensure the applicability of the statistical tests. All statistical tests are conducted on a significance level $p = 0.05$.

The experimental average values of execution time, error, and mean absolute force for the selected levels of guidance are shown in Tables 5.1 and 5.2.

Goal-directed Guidance

The performance measures for goal-directed guidance are shown in Fig. 5.7 and Table 5.1.

Execution Time: Regarding force control FC A, execution time improves with increasing assistance level. The pattern of P and C is less clear. The execution time for force control P tends to decrease with increasing assistance level until AL 3. For FC C, the shortest time was achieved with AL 2, which suggests a saturation for the last levels in FC P and C.

A two-factorial repeated ANOVA was conducted to investigate the influence of assistance level and force control method on execution time. The factor *force control* has a significant effect $(p < 0.001)$ on execution time, whereas the *assistance level* factor has no significant influence. To understand the differences in execution time depending on the force control methods, (Tukey-Kramer adjusted) multiple comparison tests were performed. The execution time of FC P is significantly higher than FC A and FC C.

Average Error: The two-factorial ANOVA showed the influence of both factors, *assistance level* (p = 0.004) and *force control* $(p < 0.001)$, on error. Post-hoc multiple comparison tests were conducted separately for each force control method. For FC A, the average error of AL 4 is significantly lower than AL 2, and for FC P, the average error of AL 4 is significantly lower than AL 1. For FC P, the tendency to reduce error by increasing

85

Tab. 5.1.: Average and Standard Deviation of Experimental Results

Level	Guidance	Time (s) Average	SD	Error (m) Average	SD	Force (N) Average	SD
		Task 1: Goal-oriented Guidance					
	Active (A)						
1	8 N	24.4789	3.4406	0.0772	0.0436	5.6383	1.4430
2	10 N	24.7236	1.6152	0.1036	0.0339	8.1429	0.8202
3	13 N	22.8648	1.9509	0.0738	0.0304	10.2122	1.4167
4	15 N	21.0838	1.9725	0.0353	0.0113	10.6647	1.5861
	Passive (P)						
1	75 Ns/m	31.5932	10.5644	0.1641	0.0479	11.8861	1.4692
2	100 Ns/m	28.5127	4.7922	0.1654	0.0577	12.3578	0.4650
3	200 Ns/m	26.1204	1.6944	0.1519	0.0797	12.6324	2.1434
4	400 Ns/m	26.4947	1.2751	0.0922	0.0436	13.2454	1.8303
	Combined (C)						
1	8 N, 75 Ns/m	21.6711	1.9221	0.0919	0.0503	6.66076	3.2528
2	8 N, 100 Ns/m	17.2049	0.7599	0.0607	0.0250	6.82058	2.6004
3	8 N, 200 Ns/m	20.1028	2.0125	0.0298	0.0193	6.76660	2.5310
4	8 N, 400 Ns/m	22.3905	2.7760	0.0237	0.0205	8.55542	3.9935

the assistance level is also visible but there is no significant difference between assistance levels due to the high variance between participants. The multiple comparison tests between force control methods reveal that P is outperformed by A and C.

Effort: The two-way ANOVA demonstrated the influence of the factor *assistance level* ($p = 0.027$) and *force control* ($p < 0.001$) on effort. The active force applied by the guidance function, and thus human effort as well, obviously increases with the level of assistance. Nevertheless, for FC P and FC C there is no significant difference between assistance levels. However, the human effort is significantly higher for force control P than for FC A and FC C.

These results indicate that, for the targeting task, FC A and FC C outperform FC P, not only in terms of execution time and error from the target position, but also in terms of human effort.

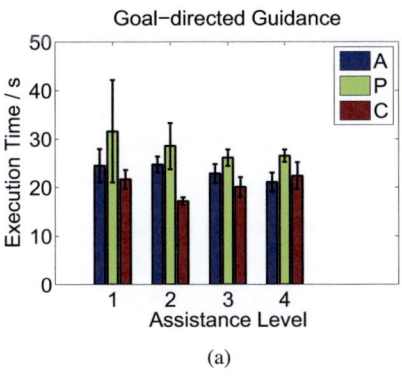

(a)

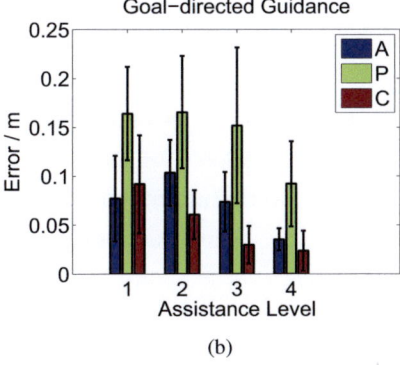

(b)

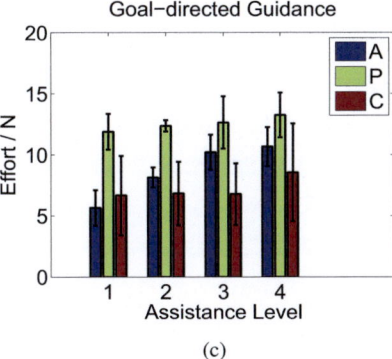

(c)

Fig. 5.5.: Mean and standard deviation of performance measures depending on assistance level and force control for goal-directed guidance.

Subjective Measures: For the targeting task, three participants preferred FC A, four participants FC C, and only one participant FC P. These subjects reported that with the active component it was much easier to find the target than with only passive guidance. Within FC A, AL 4 was preferred by four participants, AL 3 by two participants, and AL 1 by two participants. Within FC P, most participants (seven) preferred AL 4, and only one participant preferred AL 3. Within FC C, six participants liked AL 4 the most, one participant AL 3, and one participant AL 2.

Path-directed Guidance

The performance measures for path-directed guidance are shown in Fig. 5.8 and Table 5.2.

Execution Time: Regarding FC A, execution time slightly improves with increasing assistance level, whereas the execution time for FC P and FC C remains almost constant, which indicates that an increase in the level of guidance does not necessarily decrease the execution time in a path-directed task.

As in the case of goal-directed guidance, the two-factorial repeated ANOVA showed no significant influence of factor *assistance level* on execution time. The *force control* factor, by contrast, has an influence on execution time ($p < 0.001$), and multiple comparison tests again showed that FC A outperforms FC P in terms of execution time. Please note that FC C does not outperform FC P in path-directed guidance.

Path Deviation: Surprisingly, the smallest deviation from the path was achieved by FC P with AL 4. The two-way ANOVA showed influence of both factors on path deviation: *assistance level* ($p = 0.006$) and *force control* ($p < 0.001$). For FC P, the path deviation of AL 4 is significantly lower than for assistance levels AL 3 and AL 1. In addition, the multiple comparison tests revealed that FC P results in a significantly lower mean deviation than A. This is due to the fact, that with FC A the user usually leaves the path at the curves, as shown in the exemplary trajectory of Fig. 5.4.

Effort: The two-factorial ANOVA showed influence of the factor *assistance level* ($p < 0.001$) and *force control* ($p < 0.001$) on effort. For FC A, the effort of AL 1 is significantly lower than the effort of AL 3 and that of AL 4. Again, for FC P and FC C there is no significant difference between assistance levels. In addition, FC P requires significantly higher human effort than FC A and FC C.

These results indicate that FC P only outperforms FC A in terms of deviation from the reference path. However, FC A outperforms FC P in terms of execution time, and FC A and FC C require less effort than FC P.

Subjective Measures: Although most of the participants achieved greater accuracy with passive guidance, four participants preferred FC C for the path-following task, two participants preferred FC A and two participants FC P. Within FC A, four participants chose AL 1, two participants chose AL 3, and two participants AL 4. As in the previous task, within FC P, seven participants chose AL 4, and one participant AL 3. Within FC C, five participants preferred AL 4, two participants AL 3, and one participant AL 2.

These results indicate that most participants prefer high levels of guidance — levels that provide very explicit guidance — even though *very hard* active guidance produces an over-steered motion at the curves when following a path. This is not surprising, since the participants were instructed to execute the task as quickly and as accurately as possible, and since they did not have to work strongly against the haptic guidance, as it was helping them perform the task more quickly and without errors. However, in real situations, for example when dealing with unexpected obstacles, it is important that the user is able to perform the task while working against the virtual fixture.

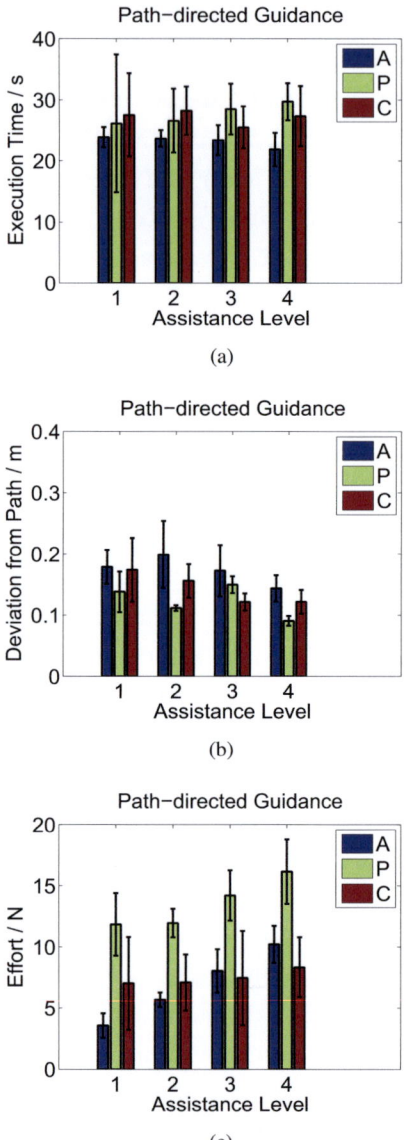

(a)

(b)

(c)

Fig. 5.6.: Mean and standard deviation of performance measures depending on assistance level and force control for path-directed guidance.

Tab. 5.2.: Average and Standard Deviation of Experimental Results

Level	Guidance	Time (s)		Error (m)		Force (N)	
		Average	SD	Average	SD	Average	SD
		Task 2: Path-directed Guidance					
	Active (A)						
1	8 N	23.9072	1.6820	0.1789	0.0279	3.5657	0.9905
2	10 N	23.7088	1.3693	0.1991	0.0549	5.6797	0.5821
3	13 N	23.4163	2.4660	0.1725	0.0420	8.0414	1.7809
4	15 N	21.8953	2.7425	0.1437	0.0214	10.2266	1.5037
	Passive (P)						
1	75 Ns/m	26.1427	11.2808	0.1380	0.0332	11.8493	2.5558
2	100 Ns/m	26.6086	5.2396	0.1114	0.0044	11.9506	1.1643
3	200 Ns/m	28.5149	4.1377	0.1497	0.0137	14.2023	2.0524
4	400 Ns/m	29.7237	3.0314	0.0906	0.0079	16.1537	2.6271
	Combined (C)						
1	8 N, 75 Ns/m	27.5495	6.8044	0.1741	0.0523	7.0150	3.7930
2	8 N, 100 Ns/m	28.2573	3.9347	0.1559	0.0273	7.0822	2.3001
3	8 N, 200 Ns/m	25.5257	3.4670	0.1214	0.0139	7.4464	3.8602
4	8 N, 400 Ns/m	27.3431	4.9313	0.1218	0.0194	8.3418	2.4556

5.4.3. Towards Adaptable Haptic Assistance

Through curve fitting, static relationships between assistance level and performance measures can be found [78]. Furthermore, a combined criterion can be used as in [87], which represents a weighted combination of the performance measures, in order to find an optimal force control method and assistance level for each navigation task.

First, an optimization criterion is formulated as the weighted sum of the objective performance measures. To do this, the performance measures have to be normalized (i.e., divided by the maximum value of the measure in the dataset). The assistance level of guidance has to be normalized as well, so that all the levels (for all force control methods A, P, and C) are mapped to a factor $\alpha \in \{0,1\}$, such that $\alpha = 0$ for AL 1 (*soft* guidance) and $\alpha = 1$ for AL 4 (*very hard* guidance).

The combined performance criterion is formulated as the weighted sum of the normalized measures

$$C = w_1 NT + w_2 ND + w_3 NE \quad : \alpha \tag{5.25}$$

where NT is the *normalized execution time*; ND is the *normalized error* in the case of goal-directed guidance, and the *normalized deviation* in the case of path-directed guidance; and NE is the *normalized effort*. w_1, w_2, and w_3 are the corresponding weighting factors. The combined criterion should be minimized in order to find the optimal guidance parameters. The sought optimal level of guidance fulfills

$$\alpha_{opt} = \arg\min_{\alpha} \{C\} \; . \tag{5.26}$$

The sought factor obviously depends on the weighting factors. Fig. 5.7(a), Fig. 5.7(b), and Fig. 5.7(c) show the fitted combined criterion for goal-directed guidance using quadratic polynomials when the combined criterion coincides with one of the normalized performance measures: time, error, and effort, respectively. These plots illustrate how the optimum value changes for each force control method by weighting the performance measures differently. Fig. 5.9(a) also shows the combined criterion using quadratic polynomials and identical weighting factors for the three normalized measures: $w_1 = 1/3$, $w_2 = 1/3$, $w_3 = 1/3$.

Analogously, Fig. 5.8(a), Fig. 5.8(b), and Fig. 5.8(c) show the fitted combined criterion for path-directed guidance when the combined criterion coincides with each of the normalized performance measures, and Fig. 5.9(b) shows the combined criterion using identical weighting factors $w_1 = 1/3$, $w_2 = 1/3$, $w_3 = 1/3$.

We did not find evidence of any linear relationship between the combined criterion and the guidance factor, except for the passive force control method, in which this relationship is almost linear. The minimum combined criterion for both goal-directed and path-directed guidance, is achieved for the combined force control method with $\alpha \approx 0.55$ ($F_G = 8$ N, $D_\perp \approx 250$ Ns/m) and $\alpha \approx 0.6$ ($F_G = 8$ N, $D_\perp \approx 270$ Ns/m), respectively.

Depending on the requirements of the navigation task, weighting factors can be assigned; and by using these approximate relationships, an adequate level of guidance can be adjusted. In fact, for error/deviation, almost monotonically decreasing relationships for all force control methods and navigation tasks were found. Similarly, monotonically increasing functions fit the effort data. Given a certain threshold of permitted error or deviation from the path, the assistance level can be adjusted (increased) online until this performance measure is within the permitted range. Analogously, the assistance level can be decreased online if the human effort exceeds a maximum permitted threshold. Furthermore, human effort can be regarded as an indication that the human is working against the guidance [87].

5.5. Summary

In this chapter, the guidance information provided by the PHGF has been transformed into haptic commands that are added to haptic information from the target scenario and presented to the user through a haptic interface.

First, guidance forces have been calculated that, when applied on the user's hand, either control the motion along the desired direction (*tracking control*) or regulate the position and orientation of the user (*posture regulation*). A kinematic and dynamic model of the user as an underactuated system was applied to derive the guidance commands.

An alternative method to using guidance forces for guiding the user towards the desired direction is favoring the motion of the user in the preferred direction or, equivalently, restricting his/her motion towards other directions. This method is called *passive force control*, in order to distinguish it from *active force control*, which guides the user by means of guidance forces. Both force control methods, *active* and *passive*, can be combined.

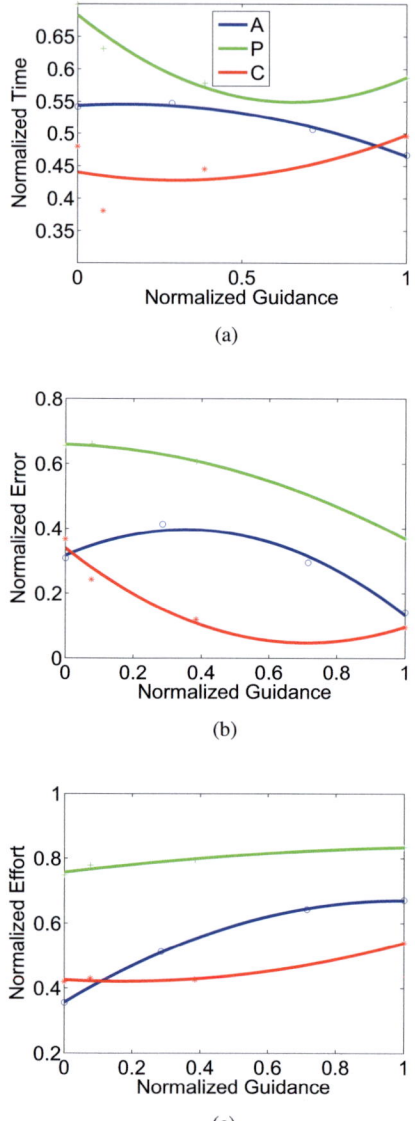

Fig. 5.7.: Polynomials fitted to normalized performance measures for goal-directed guidance.

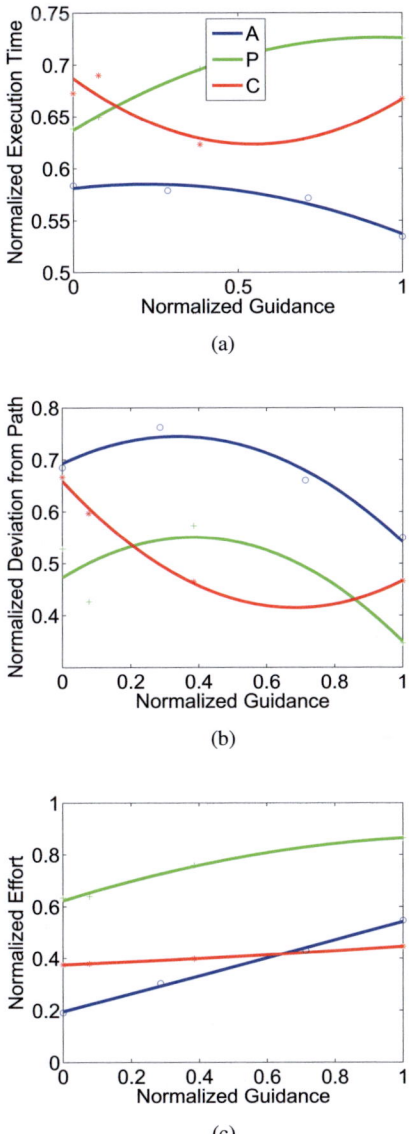

(a)

(b)

(c)

Fig. 5.8.: Polynomials fitted to normalized performance measures for path-directed guidance.

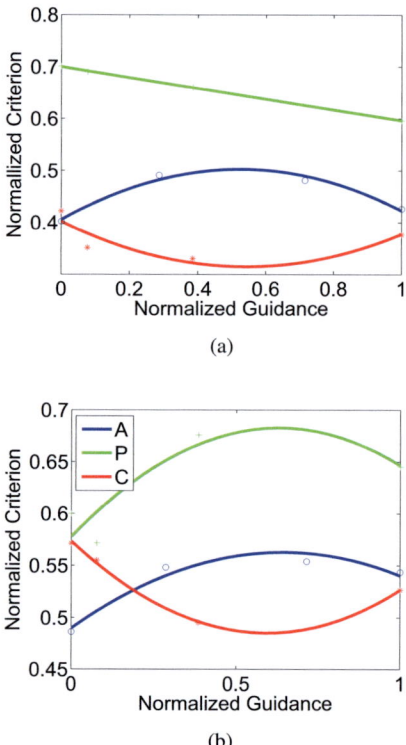

Fig. 5.9.: Polynomials fitted to combined performance criterion with weights $a_1 = 1/3$, $a_2 = 1/3$, $a_3 = 1/3$. (a) Goal-directed guidance.   (b) Path-directed guidance.

The parametrization of the force control methods determines the strength of the haptic guidance. An experimental evaluation has been performed in order to identify the most adequate force control method and its parameters for two elementary navigation tasks that require goal-directed and path-directed guidance. Moreover, static relationships between the assistance level and several performance measures have been identified based on gathered experimental data. These relationships allow us to predict user performance depending on the assistance level and the force control method, as well to adjust the optimal assistance level depending on the task requirements. The experiments were performed with the semi-mobile haptic interface whose control and realization are the focus of Chapter 6 and Chapter 7, respectively.

6. Design and Control of Semi-mobile Haptic Interfaces

A haptic interface is a bidirectional human-system interface that reads the motion and force input of the operator and simultaneously displays defined forces to the operator. In our extended range telepresence system, the haptic interface displays not only contact forces from the remote environment but also haptic information so as to guide the user in both the target environment and the user environment. Such an interface faces several challenges: First, the haptic information has to be displayed over the whole user environment; second, the information has to be displayed while the user is walking; and third, the information has to be perceived by the user in an intuitive way.

However, most of the available haptic interfaces have a small workspace and a low output capability. Only a few of them, in particular exoskeletons and mobile haptic interfaces, are adequate for extended range telepresence. However, as reported in Chapter 2, these haptic interfaces also present some drawbacks. Therefore, in this work, a novel type of haptic interfaces called *semi-mobile haptic interfaces* (SMHIs) [106, 145] is used to achieve wide-area user guidance.

In this chapter, we present the design and the control of a new semi-mobile haptic interface that makes it possible to enlarge the workspace and to simplify the motion control of the haptic interface. In addition, a stability analysis has been performed in order to investigate the effects of the dynamic properties of the SMHI on the stability of the controlled system.

6.1. Design of Semi-mobile Haptic Interfaces

Since wide-area locomotion and force display demand very different properties, *semi-mobile haptic interfaces* (SMHIs) consist of two subsystems
[107]:

- a wide-area prepositioning unit (PPU) with a large workspace, which
  follows the user's motion,

- and a fast haptic manipulator (HM) with a small workspace, which
  provides haptic feedback to the user.

The workspace of the PPU must coincide with the area in which the user
can move, i.e., the user environment, which is generally limited either by
the range of the tracking system or by the available space in the room. The
smaller this workspace, the higher the resulting path curvature and, consequently, the higher the inconsistencies in the perceived information from
the target environment. Furthermore, it is convenient for the rotation of
the end-effector around the vertical axis to be unconstrained. This characteristic reduces the necessary movements of the PPU and permits better
utilization of the user environment since the user can walk around the PPU.

The main duty of the PPU is to follow the motion of the user. Therefore,
the PPU has to be fast, maneuverable, and omnidirectional. The PPU has
to resist the high forces transmitted by the haptic manipulator without over-
balancing. Moreover, the position of the PPU has to be accurately known
with respect to a world coordinate system. Therefore, the SMHI uses a
grounded Cartesian robot as a PPU because of its simplicity, rigidity, and
high position accuracy.

The purpose of the HM is to measure the user's hand position and to
accurately display forces. For a high-fidelity haptic feedback, the HM requires, on the one hand, a human-like output capability in order to follow
the fast motions of the user's hand and to display high contact forces, and on
the other hand, the HM requires the exact measurement of the end-effector

position so that the force control can compensate for the dynamics of the haptic interface.

In order to successfully decouple the motion of the PPU from the motion of the HM, the workspace of the HM either needs to be similar to the workspace of the human arm or, in the best-case scenario, coincident with it. For this reason, a new setup configuration for the SMHI has been designed. Two system configurations for the SMHI are possible (cf. Fig. 6.1), and these two will henceforth be called *frontal configuration* and *mirror configuration*.

In the standard *frontal configuration*, which is illustrated in Fig. 6.1(a), the human operator interacts head-on with the system, so that the device is opposite the operator. A first prototype of an SMHI with this configuration was first presented in [107, 145]. In the new *mirror configuration*, which is illustrated in Fig. 6.1(b), the human is enclosed by the system and the SMHI mirrors the motion of the user, which delivers several benefits with respect to the former configuration.

The new configuration is more ergonomic because it covers the human arm's planar workspace better. Since the human operator is situated under the haptic manipulator, the operator's body occupies the non-reachable workspace of the haptic manipulator. In fact, a study presented in [130] showed that, for a fixed haptic device, the workspace coverage values were better in a configuration in which the robot arm encloses the human arm than in a configuration in which the robot arm is opposite the human operator.

In addition, the danger of the PPU hindering the human motion is considerably reduced with the *mirror configuration*. This is very important in a system for extended range telepresence, since the PPU and the human operator share the workspace without the human operator being aware of the motion of the PPU. Please note that this problem also exists when using mobile haptic interfaces. Furthermore, with this configuration, a better utilization of the available space in the user environment is achieved by using

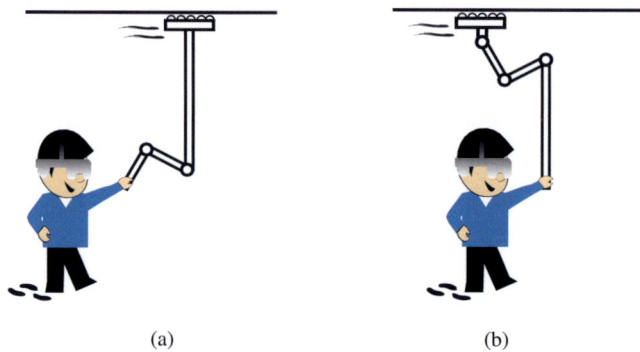

(a)   (b)

Fig. 6.1.: Two possible system configurations for the SMHI. (a) In the *frontal configuration*, the haptic manipulator is opposite the user. (b) In the *mirror configuration*, the haptic manipulator is atop the user and reflects his/her motion.

a simple prepositioning algorithm (cf. Section 6.5) to decouple the motion of the PPU and the HM.

6.2. Control of the Semi-mobile Haptic Interfaces

6.2.1. Control Overview

As explained in Section 3.1, there are two haptic control loops closed on the user: the control loop for telepresent manipulation, and the control loop for telepresent motion with haptic assistance, both of which are based on visual, proprioceptive, and haptic stimuli. Fig. 6.2 shows the haptic control loops in detail. As in the rest of this work, the subscript $(\cdot)_U$ refers to the information in the user environment, and $(\cdot)_T$ to the same information (transformed) in the target environment.

In the manipulation control loop, the position of the end-effector of the haptic interface $\underline{x}_{E,U}$, which coincides with the position of the user's hand, is transformed and sent to the target environment as $\underline{x}_{E,T}$. In the target environment, the motion of the user's hand results in interaction forces from the target environment $\underline{F}_T$, which are transformed back into the user environment and displayed by the haptic interface.

At the same time, within the haptic assistance loop, the current position of the human operator $\underline{x}_{H,U}$ is tracked in the user environment, transformed into the target environment, and sent to the proxy. The current pose of the proxy $\underline{x}_{H,T}$ together with context information from the target environment (e.g., position of intended goals and obstacles) are used to calculate the PHGF, which, depending on the force control method, can be rendered as a guidance force $\underline{F}_G$ or as a high compliance towards the desired guidance direction $\underline{d}_T$.

Both control loops use the same haptic interface to present the haptic information to the user, so that the guidance force $\underline{F}_G$ is added to the contact force from the target environment $\underline{F}_T$ resulting the reference force $\underline{F}_{ref,T}$. In order to provide consistent information in both environments, the guidance direction $\underline{d}_T$ and the reference force $\underline{F}_{ref,T}$ are transformed with Motion Compression into the user environment and sent to the haptic interface.

This scheme represents a bilateral telepresence system with *position-force exchange* [9,48] in which positions are sent to the target environment, and target forces are sent back to the user. In this system the target environment is modeled as an *impedance*, i.e., the target forces $\underline{F}_T$ result from the user's hand motion $\underline{x}_{E,T}$. By contrast, the haptic interface is modeled as an *admittance*, since the motion of the haptic manipulator $\underline{x}_{E,U}$ is derived from the resultant force acting on the end-effector (the sum of the reference force $\underline{F}_{ref,U}$ and the force applied by the user $\underline{F}_{H,U}$), according to the desired admittance model given by $C(\underline{d}_U)$.

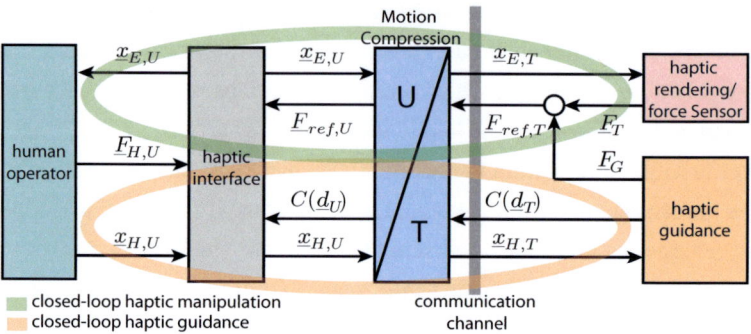

Fig. 6.2.: Overall haptic control of the extended range telepresence system with haptic guidance.

6.2.2. Control Schemes with Drift Compensation

In the telepresence system with *position-force exchange* described above, the reference force at the haptic interface $\underline{F}_{ref,U}$ is the force transformed from the target environment as

$$\underline{F}_{ref,U} = {}^{OU}\mathbf{T}_{OT} \cdot \underline{F}_{ref,T} , \tag{6.1}$$

where ${}^{OU}\mathbf{T}_{OT}$ is the inverse instantaneous transformation provided by Motion Compression (cf. Section 3.3). This transformation results in a rotation of the force such that the magnitude of the force is identical in both environments.

However, by using the alternative two-channel bilateral control scheme, i.e., the *force-position exchange* [66], in which forces are sent from the user side to teleoperator and positions are sent from the teleoperator to the haptic interface, special attention has to be paid, since the velocity of the user's hand is not the same in the user and the target environments due to Motion Compression.

As explained in Section 3.4, the velocity of the user's hand in the user environment is, due to the difference of path curvature, generally different from the velocity of the proxy's end-effector in the target environment. Thus, in order to track the desired velocity of the proxy's end-effector in the target environment, the commanded velocity of the haptic interface in the user environment should be

$$\underline{\dot{x}}_{E,ref,U} = {}^{OU}\mathbf{T}_{OT} \cdot \underline{\dot{x}}_{E,ref,T} (1 + n \cdot \Delta \kappa) \,, \tag{6.2}$$

where $\underline{\dot{x}}_{E,ref,T}$ is the desired velocity of the proxy's end-effector in the target environment, n is the signed normal distance between the user's hand and the user path (which is positive towards the outward-pointing normal to the curved user path), and $\Delta \kappa = \kappa_U - \kappa_T$ is the instantaneous curvature difference between the user and target paths.

Alternatively, in order to specify the desired end-effector motion from the target environment, it is possible to extend the previous *position-force exchange* control scheme by adding a velocity feedback term with gain K_p, which results in an additional force $\underline{F}_v$ such that

$$\underline{F}_v = K_p \left(\underline{\dot{x}}_{E,ref,U} - \underline{\dot{x}}_{E,U} \right) = K_p \left({}^{OU}\mathbf{T}_{OT} \cdot \underline{\dot{x}}_{E,ref,T} (1 + n \cdot \Delta \kappa) - \underline{\dot{x}}_{E,U} \right) \,, \tag{6.3}$$

and the total force to be displayed by the manipulator becomes

$$\underline{F}_{ref,U} = {}^{OU}\mathbf{T}_{OT} \cdot \underline{F}_{ref,T} + \underline{F}_v \,. \tag{6.4}$$

Please note that this extended control law corresponds to a four-channel controller [73].

6.3. Redundancy Resolution of Haptic Interface

The main idea behind the control of the haptic device is the separation between wide-area motion and haptic interaction. The display of the target
impedance and the guidance commands is performed by the haptic manipulator (HM), while the prepositioning unit (PPU) translates the HM with
the user's motion, so that the user never leaves the workspace of the manipulator. The separation is only possible for the planar redundant DOFs,
which are present in both the PPU and the HM.

The pose of the end-effector with respect to the world coordinate system
$^O\mathbf{T}_E$ can be expressed in terms of the pose of the linear PPU in the world
coordinate system $^O\mathbf{T}_L$, which is completely defined by the configuration
of the PPU, and the pose of the end-effector with respect to the PPU $^L\mathbf{T}_E$,
which depends only on the configuration γ of the haptic manipulator as

$$^O\mathbf{T}_E = {}^O\mathbf{T}_L \cdot {}^L\mathbf{T}_E \;, \tag{6.5}$$

so that the position of the end-effector can be expressed as

$$\underline{x}_E = \underline{x}_L + \underline{x}_S \;. \tag{6.6}$$

The control architecture of the haptic interface is displayed in Fig. 6.3.
The subscript $(\cdot)_U$ has been removed for simplicity, since all variables here
belong to the user environment. The haptic manipulator is admittance-
controlled, i.e., the device motion is controlled to display the desired force
$\underline{F}_{ref}$ and the admittance $C(\underline{d})$. The output of the admittance model is the
reference position of the motion controller, which calculates the required
torques of the haptic manipulator. The motion controller also takes the acceleration of the PPU into account in order to compensate for the dynamics
of the PPU.

According to (6.5) and due to the planar redundant DOFs, the haptic
interface has, for the given end-effector position $\underline{x}_E$, infinite solutions for

the positions $\underline{x}_S$ and $\underline{x}_L$. This redundancy can be solved by calculating, for the current end-effector position $\underline{x}_E$, the position of the PPU that optimizes the configuration of the haptic manipulator according to a certain quality criterion, e.g., the manipulability of the haptic manipulator. A similar approach was used in [82] for a mobile haptic interface. In our approach, the position of the user $\underline{x}_H$ is also used to calculate the optimal configuration of the manipulator $\underline{\gamma}^*$ [145, 147]. This calculation of the PPU position on the basis of the end-effector position is called *prepositioning algorithm*. In Section 6.5, we present different prepositioning algorithms that depend on the setup configuration of the semi-mobile haptic interface.

The position of the PPU, which optimizes the configuration of the manipulator, is given by

$$\underline{x}_{L,ref} = \underline{x}_E - \underline{x}_S^* , \tag{6.7}$$

where $\underline{x}_S^* = \underline{x}_S(\underline{\gamma}^*)$ is the optimal position of the end-effector with respect to the PPU, and $\underline{x}_{L,ref}$ is the input of the position control of the PPU. As a result of the prepositioning algorithm, the PPU moves in the null space of the haptic interface.

Since the bandwidth of the PPU is much lower than the bandwidth of the HM, fast end-effector motions are undertaken by the manipulator, while slow end-effector motions can be followed by the PPU. One approach for explicitly assigning fast motions to the manipulator consists in placing a low pass filter on the end-effector position before the position is fed into the prepositioning algorithm. For semi-mobile haptic interfaces with the *mirror configuration*, a prepositioning algorithm is presented that directly assigns the user's motion to the PPU and the user's hand motion to the HM.

6.4. Control of Haptic Manipulator

The force control of the haptic manipulator controls the motion-force relation between operator and the haptic interface. By controlling the haptic

107

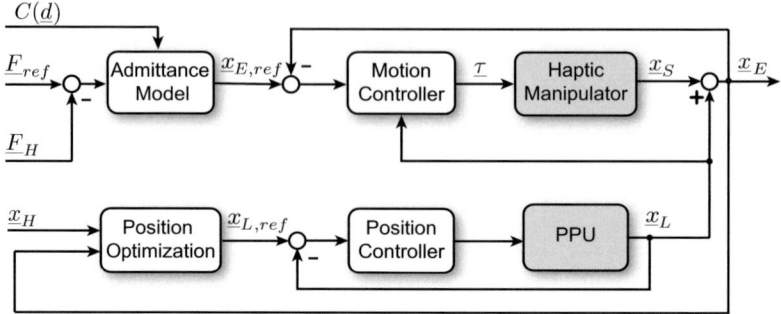

Fig. 6.3.: Control overview of the haptic interface.

interface in the admittance display mode, the device motion is controlled based on force input [122]. Admittance control is required for passive guidance and transparent force display with a semi-mobile haptic interface with large dynamic properties.

The haptic display is modeled as an admittance that transforms the external forces — i.e., the reference force $\underline{F}_{ref}$ from the target environment and the force applied by the user $\underline{F}_H$, which is measured by a force-torque sensor — into the desired motion of the end-effector. The admittance model describes the desired motion of the end-effector under the influence of the external forces as follows:

$$\underline{F}_{ref} - \underline{F}_H = \mathbf{M_m}(\underline{d})\underline{\ddot{x}}_{E,ref} + \mathbf{D_m}(\underline{d})\underline{\dot{x}}_{E,ref} + \mathbf{K_m}(\underline{d})\underline{x}_{E,ref}, \qquad (6.8)$$

where $\mathbf{M_m}$ is the mass matrix of the displayed virtual object, and $\mathbf{D_m}$ and $\mathbf{K_m}$ are matrices that represent the viscous damping and the stiffness of the environment, respectively. For passive guidance, the directional admittance model, which depends on the preferred guidance direction $\underline{d}$ is updated at each time-step. The minimum target inertia that can be shown in free motion is limited by stability.

The reference position of the end-effector $x_{E,ref}$ is the input of the motion controller, in this case a *computed torque motion controller*, which calculates the desired torques $\underline{\tau}$ of the haptic manipulator. The computed torque motion controller linearizes and decouples the manipulator dynamics in a series of double integrators. It consists of a block amplifying the control error (e.g., a PD position controller) with an acceleration feed-forward term and a block converting the output signal to commanded motor torque, which can be considered as an open-loop acceleration control law [122]. The control law of this motion controller is given by

$$\underline{\tau} = \hat{\mathbf{M}}_\gamma \mathbf{J}^{-1}\left(\underline{\gamma}\right)\underline{\ddot{x}}_C + \hat{\underline{h}}\left(\underline{\gamma},\underline{\dot{\gamma}}\right) + \mathbf{J}^T \underline{F}_H \,, \qquad (6.9)$$

where $\underline{\ddot{x}}_C$ is the commanded acceleration, $\hat{\mathbf{M}}_\gamma$ is an approximation of the device joint inertia matrix, $\hat{\underline{h}}$ is an approximation of the friction forces (both were approximated through experimental identification), and $\mathbf{J}$ is the Jacobian of the manipulator. Adding the sensed force mapped into the joint space to the input of the acceleration controller aims at a compensation of the force applied by the operator. This force feed-forward can greatly reduce position errors due to interaction forces.

The commanded manipulator's Cartesian acceleration is calculated as

$$\underline{\ddot{x}}_C = \underline{\ddot{x}}_{S,ref} + \mathbf{K}_p\left(\underline{x}_{S,ref} - \underline{x}_S\right) + \mathbf{K}_d\left(\underline{\dot{x}}_{S,ref} - \underline{\dot{x}}_S\right) \,, \qquad (6.10)$$

where $\mathbf{K}_p$ and $\mathbf{K}_d$ denote the position and velocity gain matrices, respectively. They are usually chosen with $\mathbf{K}_p = \omega^2 \mathbf{I}$ and $\mathbf{K}_d = 2\zeta\omega\mathbf{I}$, where ω is the desired bandwidth and ζ the desired damping ratio of the position control.

Please note that the motion control of the manipulator has to be done using the position of the end-effector with respect to the PPU, which is $\underline{x}_S = \underline{x}_E - \underline{x}_L$. Given the reference position of the end-effector from the admittance model $\underline{x}_{E,ref}$, the change of coordinates in the local coordinate system is done by using the current position of the PPU as

$$\underline{x}_{S,ref} = \underline{x}_{E,ref} - \underline{x}_L .$$ (6.11)

By introducing (6.11) into (6.10), the commanded acceleration is given by

$$\underline{\ddot{x}}_C = \underline{\ddot{x}}_{E,ref} - \underline{\ddot{x}}_L + \mathbf{K}_p \left(\underline{x}_{E,ref} - \underline{x}_E \right) + \mathbf{K}_d \left(\underline{\dot{x}}_{E,ref} - \underline{\dot{x}}_E \right) .$$ (6.12)

Please note that the term $\underline{\ddot{x}}_{E,ref} - \underline{\ddot{x}}_L$ of the motion controller accounts for the compensation of the dynamic effects due to the motion of the PPU. The same controller can be used for semi-mobile haptic interfaces with both setup configurations. In fact, the main difference between the two configurations is that the frontal setup configuration introduces a certain flexibility in the system due to the presence of the long last link. However, according to the theory of flexible manipulators [118], the same PD controller designed for the rigid system also stabilizes the manipulator with a flexible link.

6.5. Control of Prepositioning Unit

The purpose of the prepositioning algorithm is to solve the redundancy of the system by driving the haptic manipulator into a convenient configuration that satisfies certain conditions expressed as cost functions. These conditions aim at keeping the haptic device away from its singularities and guarantee the motion freedom and the safety of the user. Furthermore, fast movements of the PPU, which can cause undesired inertial forces, have to be avoided by the prepositioning algorithm.

Because all configurations of the PPU are equally valid, the optimization of the configuration of the haptic interface is equivalent to the optimization of the configuration of the haptic manipulator. In general, this optimization does not rely on a preplanned path, but only on the current positions of the user and the end-effector and on the current direction of motion. Naturally, the optimal propositioning of the PPU depends on the setup configuration of the semi-mobile haptic interface.

6.5.1. Prepositioning of Frontal Configuration

The first step of the optimization strategy is designed to maximize the manipulability of the haptic manipulator, e.g., velocity manipulability [145]. The optimal configuration $\underline{\gamma}^*$ that maximizes the manipulability $w(\underline{\gamma})$ satisfies

$$\underline{\gamma}^* = \arg\max_{\underline{\gamma}} \left\{ w(\underline{\gamma}) \right\}, \tag{6.13}$$

where $w(\underline{\gamma})$ represents the manipulability of the haptic manipulator.

In order to illustrate the following prepositioning algorithms, a 2DOFs parallel manipulator with four links (like the one described in Chapter 7) is assumed. However, these prepositioning algorithms can easily be adapted to other kinematics (with more DOFs) by using the planar DOFs for the prepositioning. The manipulability of the assumed haptic manipulator is only affected by the radial distance between the end-effector and the PPU, i.e., $\|\underline{x}_S\|$, which is constant on circles around the PPU of radius R_{opt}^*. With this criterion, the desired position of the PPU $\underline{x}_{L,ref}$ is not completely specified yet, so that another criterion is required, and the position of the user has to be taken into account so that the PPU does not interfere with his/her motion. Two algorithms have been proposed on this account.

The first of these algorithms places the PPU at the most distant position from the user that still satisfies that maximum manipulability condition from (6.13) [145]. By using this algorithm, the distance between the

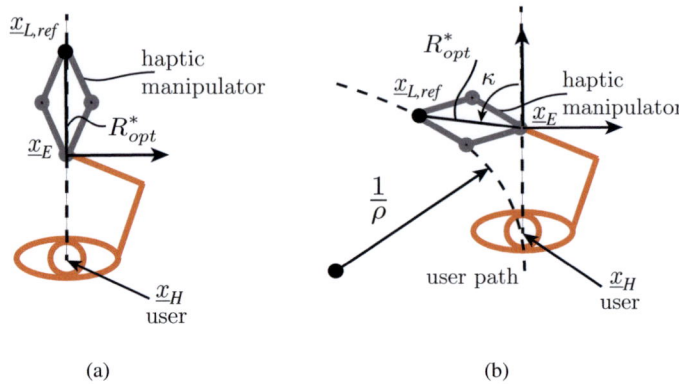

(a)   (b)

Fig. 6.4.: Two prepositioning algorithms for the SMHI with frontal setup configuration based on optimal manipulability. (a) The PPU is prepositioned at
the maximum distance from the user. (b) The PPU is prepositioned by
considering the instantaneous path curvature.

user and the PPU is maximized by placing the PPU on the connecting line
between the user and the user's hand as

$$\underline{x}_{L,ref} = \underline{x}_E - R^*_{opt} \frac{\underline{x}_H - \underline{x}_E}{\|\underline{x}_H - \underline{x}_E\|} \, . \tag{6.14}$$

Fig. 6.4(a) illustrates this approach. The problem of this solution is that
it leaves a lot of space in the user environment unutilized, since the user has
to walk inside the workspace of the haptic interface at a certain distance
from the limits of the workspace — a distance which is larger than any
maximum distance between the user and the PPU — so that the PPU can
fulfill the prepositioning routine. By reducing the available area in which
the user can walk, the curvature of the user path generally increases, as do,
similarly, the perceived sensory inconsistencies. For this reason, another
prepositioning algorithm has been proposed [147] that maximizes the space
in the user environment in which the user can freely walk.

Fig. 6.4(b) illustrates the idea of the new approach. The key concept of this algorithm is the approximation of the current curvature of the user path (using the user's current direction of motion) and the calculation of the reference position of the PPU that adjusts itself to the curvature of the path. For this purpose, the user is assumed to walk forwards, which is a realistic assumption when Motion Compression is used. While following a piecewise straight path in the arbitrarily large target environment, the user walks tangential to a curved user path in the user environment. The angle κ in Fig. 6.4(b) depends on the instantaneous path curvature $\frac{1}{\rho}$ and on the current direction of motion of the user's hand. By prepositioning the PPU in such a way that the angle at the hand position is κ (please note that for the maximum distance approach as well as for a straight user path this angle would be $\kappa = 0$), the PPU will always be prepositioned towards the curved path.

The instantaneous path transformation provided by Motion Compression is not directly used in order to transform the position of the PPU to a feasible position on the user path, since this transformation can change too rapidly and does not account for the user's arm motions. Instead, a smooth approximation of the path curvature based on the current motion data of the user in the user environment is used, which produces a smooth motion of the PPU.

By combining both the motion of the user and the motion of the user's hand, this method succeeds in adjusting the motion of the PPU to the current curvature of the user path, as well as in following the fast motions of the user's hand around his/her body, which obviously leads, as in the case of the maximum distance approach, to fast rotations of the PPU around the user. In [147], an experimental comparison between both prepositioning algorithms is presented.

6.5.2. Prepositioning of Mirror Configuration

The mirror setup configuration of the semi-mobile haptic interface considerably simplifies the prepositioning algorithm. In order to illustrate this, let us once again consider the planar manipulator from the previous section. Since the planar workspace of the haptic manipulator and the human's arm have a similar form (which is approximately the section of a hollow cylinder), the position of the PPU that best covers the workspace of the human arm is the one that is coincident with the user position, i.e., the position at which the PPU is exactly above the user.

The prepositioning algorithm that keeps the PPU above the user has two further benefits. On the one hand, it avoids fast motions of the PPU, since the PPU only follows the (generally slower) motions of the user's body (compared to the motions of the user's arm); and on the other hand, the utilization of the user environment is optimal, since the user can reach all positions within the workspace of the semi-mobile haptic interface.

All the same, special attention must be paid to the situation wherein the user holds the end-effector near the boundaries of his/her own workspace. For this purpose, an optimal region is defined in which the manipulability of the manipulator (e.g., the velocity manipulability or the isotropy of the force output) is within a certain optimal range (e.g., the isotropy of the force output is higher than 80%). Since the manipulability of the assumed haptic manipulator is only affected by the radial distance R between the end-effector and the PPU, this optimum region is defined by R^*_{min} and R^*_{max}.

If the end-effector leaves this optimal region, e.g., if the human bends his/her arm closed toward his/her body or completely stretches his/her arm, then the PPU is shifted in the end-effector's current direction of motion.

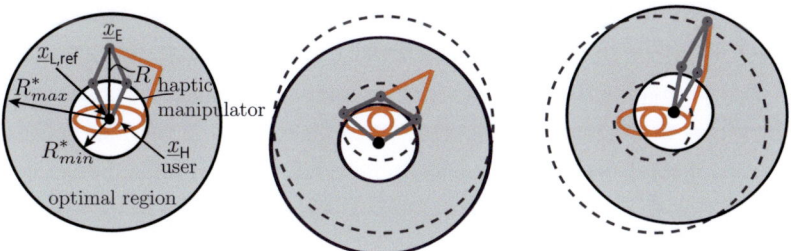

Fig. 6.5.: Prepositioning algorithm for the SMHI with mirror setup configuration.

The following mapping between the position of the user and the reference position of the PPU is performed:

$$
\underline{x}_{L,ref} =
\begin{cases}
\underline{x}_H + S_{in} \left(R^*_{min} - R \right) \frac{\underline{x}_H - \underline{x}_E}{\|\underline{x}_H - \underline{x}_E\|} & \text{if } R < R^*_{min} \\
\underline{x}_H & \text{if } R^*_{min} < R < R^*_{max} \ , \\
\underline{x}_H + S_{out} \left(R^*_{max} - R \right) \frac{\underline{x}_H - \underline{x}_E}{\|\underline{x}_H - \underline{x}_E\|} & \text{if } R > R^*_{max}
\end{cases}
$$

$$(6.15)$$

where S_{in} and S_{out} are scaling factors of the shift, which can take values between *zero* and *one*. If S_{in} or S_{out} is smaller than *one*, the position shift still allows the end-effector to abandon the optimal region. If they are *zero*, no shift is performed. Fig. 6.5 shows the possible situations that can occur during the operation. The dashed circles represent the nominal position of the optimal region at which the PPU would be situated exactly above the user.

6.6. Stability Analysis

6.6.1. Model of Linear 1 DOF SMHI

As is well known, the minimum inertia (target mass m_d and damping b_d) displayable by an admittance-controlled haptic interface simulating free motion is bounded by stability. In this section, the effect of the PPU on the stability of the haptic interface, which distinguishes the semi-mobile haptic interface from other conventional haptic interfaces, and the effect of an increment in the compliance of the haptic manipulator, are analyzed. The effect of the manipulator compliance on stability is relevant because the mirror setup configuration usually introduces a certain flexibility compared to the frontal setup configuration, due to the presence of the long last link in the manipulator.

On this account, a simplified linear one-DOF model is assumed for the haptic interface as well as human operator, and the stability is analyzed by testing the asymptotic stability of the overall system, as in [81, 91]. The haptic interface is modeled as a mass-damper system as shown in Fig. 6.6. A compliant model as proposed in [81] was used. In our study the mass and damping of the mobile platform are replaced with those of the PPU m_p and b_p. Since the stiffness of the PPU is very high and the position measurements are very accurate and taken directly at the PPU side, the stiffness k_p of the PPU can be neglected. The compliant model of the manipulator is represented by two masses, m_1 and m_2, and assumes that the compliance of the manipulator is concentrated in a single spring-damper system c_m, b_{m2}. Here, f_m is the force applied by the motor of the manipulator.

Since the user interacts with the haptic interface, a model of the human arm is also needed. A model according to [74] is used, where m_h denotes the human arm mass, c_h the human arm stiffness, and b_h the human arm damping. The factor $\alpha \in [0, 1]$ is used to take the variable human arm impedance into account, as in [91]. The exogenous force applied by the human operator is modeled by f_h. Finally m_e denotes the end-effector mass, and f_s the force measured by the force sensor located at the end-effector.

This system is represented by the series of differential equations as

$$0 = f_h + f_s - (\alpha m_h + m_e)\ddot{x}_{m2} - \alpha b_h \dot{x}_{m2} - \alpha c_h x_{m2} ,$$
$$0 = f_s + m_{m2}\ddot{x}_{m2} + b_{m2}(\dot{x}_{m2} - \dot{x}_{m1}) + c_m(x_{m2} - x_{m1}) ,$$
$$0 = -f_m + m_1\ddot{x}_{m1} - b_{m2}(\dot{x}_{m2} - \dot{x}_{m1}) - c_m(x_{m2} - x_{m1}) - b_{m1}(\dot{x}_p - \dot{x}_{m1}) ,$$
$$0 = f_m + b_{m1}(\dot{x}_p - \dot{x}_{m1}) + b_p\dot{x}_p + m_p\ddot{x}_p .$$

$$(6.16)$$

In order to reproduce effects visible in the real hardware experiment, the non-ideal actuator and the sensor dynamics have to be considered. For example the electrical time constant T_a induced by the electrical motors is modeled by a low-pass filter

$$f_m = \hat{f}_m \frac{1}{1 + sT_a} . \qquad (6.17)$$

The force signal is also filtered with a low-pass filter such that

$$\hat{f}_s = \hat{f}_s \frac{1}{1 + sT_f} , \qquad (6.18)$$

where T_f is the time constant of the force sensor.

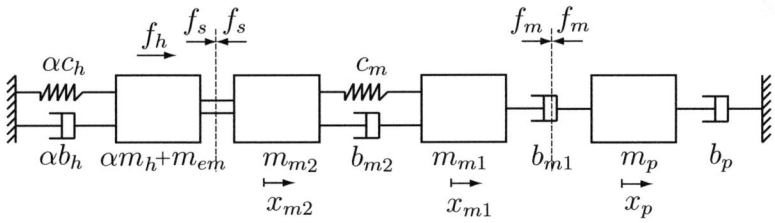

Fig. 6.6.: Compliant model of semi-mobile haptic interface and human.

6.6.2. Stability Analysis

Using the presented models, asymptotic stability is analyzed for the admittance controlled haptic interface. The cross-couplings are assumed to be compensated for by the motion controller, and the position controllers are assumed to be tuned so that

$$\hat{f}_m = K_d(\dot{x}_{E,ref} - \dot{x}_E) + K_p(x_{E,ref} - x_E) , \qquad (6.19)$$

and

$$-\hat{f}_s = m_d\ddot{x}_{E,ref} + b_d\dot{x}_{E,ref} , \qquad (6.20)$$

whereby K_d and K_p denote the control parameters of the position controller, and m_d and b_d are the minimum mass and damping needed to guarantee stability. Since the measurement of the end-effector position is performed at the motor side and the constant of the encoders is negligible, it is assumed that $x_E = x_{m1}$.

The position of the PPU is controlled to follow the motion of the user and the manipulator's end-effector. In the most general case, the PPU follows the motion of the end-effector (x_{m1}), and the position control of the PPU can be represented as

$$\dot{x}_p = K_{pp}(x_{m1} - x_p) , \qquad (6.21)$$

where K_{pp} is the gain of the position controller of the PPU.

These equations are transformed into Laplace space. The input of the system is the human force f_h, and the output the end-effector position x_E. The stability analysis thus considers the transfer function $G(s) = \frac{X_E(s)}{F_H(s)}$. For linear systems stability is equivalent to the condition that the real part of the zeros of the characteristic polynomial are negative. In the case of contact, the position control of the manipulator is simplified to a fixed value control, which is always stable. For this reason, the stability analysis is reduced to free motion.

The effect of the manipulator compliance was first analyzed. For this purpose a bisection algorithm is used in the parameter space given by the inverse of the minimum desired target mass m_d^{-1} and the damping b_d. Fig. 6.7 shows the simulation results for two different compliance values c_m. The parameters used in the simulation are $m_1 = 6.5$ kg, $m_2 = 6.5$ kg, $m_p = 100$ kg, $m_e = 0.35$ kg, $b_{m1} = 20$ Nsm^{-1}, $b_{m2} = 20$ Nsm^{-1}, $b_p = 20$ Nsm^{-1}, $T_a = 0.003$ s, $T_f = 0.003$ s, $K_p = 250$, $K_d = 13000$, and $K_{pp} = 500$ s^{-1}. The human operator model parameters are taken from [74]: $m_h = 5$ kg, $b_h = 6$ Nsm^{-1}, $c_h = 40$ Nm^{-1}, $\alpha = 1$.

The simulation results (cf. Fig. 6.7) show that the higher the compliance, the larger the stability region. In fact, for a compliance value of $c_m = 30000$ Nm^{-1}, the minimum m_d that can be displayed for $b_d = 0$ is $m_d = 0.3^{-1} \approx 3$ kg, whereas for a higher manipulator compliance (lower rigidity) $c_m = 3000$ Nm^{-1}, the minimum m_d that can be displayed for $b_d = 0$ is $m_d = 32^{-1} \approx 0.031$ kg. The minimum displayable inertia is a measure of *transparency* in free space, i.e., how much the user feels direct interaction with the remote environment. However, a manipulator with high compliance also limits the maximum rigidity that the system can display, and thus limits *transparency* in the case of hard contacts in the target environment. Experimental results with our setup showed that the stable region has a similar form to that of simulations, and that the minimum displayable mass for damping $b_d = 0$ is $m_d \approx 3$ kg. Further experimental results about the display quality of the prototypical setup are provided in Chapter 7.

The analysis of the transfer function $G(s) = \frac{X_E(s)}{F_H(s)}$ showed that the mass of the PPU m_p has no influence on the stability region, only on the force display quality. This happens because the PPU is very rigid and its compliance is negligible, which is a further benefit of semi-mobile haptic interfaces compared to mobile haptic interfaces, where the compliance of the mobile platform cannot be neglected. However, the gain of the position controller of the PPU does influence the stability region. Fig. 6.8 shows the simulation results for two different values of the gain K_{pp}. The stability region grows with increasing K_{pp}, i.e., with increasing stiffness of the position controller.

The effect of the mass of the haptic manipulator on the stability has also been investigated. Fig. 6.9 shows the simulation results, with all parameters except the specified ones being the same. Surprisingly, the stability region of the interface increases with higher manipulator mass (compared to Fig. 6.8(a)). However, although a lower target mass can be assigned to the admittance model, the mass that the operator actually perceives is limited by the mass of the manipulator [82], i.e., the force display quality deteriorates with increasing manipulator mass.

Finally, simulation results also showed that higher arm impedance (i.e., stiffer grasp of the user) leads to a higher required minimum mass, i.e., to a smaller stable region, which is in accordance with the experimental results. Fig. 6.10 shows how the stability region increases (compared again to Fig.6.8(a)) when human compliance is reduced in half. Similar results were reported in [91].

6.7. Summary

In this chapter, we presented a new ergonomic setup configuration for semi-mobile haptic interfaces, the *mirror configuration*, which, compared to the standard *frontal configuration*, ensures better coverage of the human workspace and increases human safety. The overall control of the telepresence system together with the control strategy of the semi-mobile haptic interface not only make possible the unrestricted operator motion in the target environment, but also the display of forces with high quality. As a result, high-fidelity extended range telepresence with wide-area haptic guidance can be achieved.

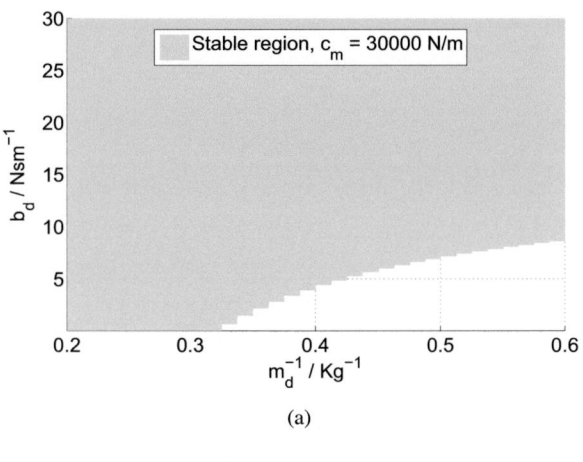

(a)

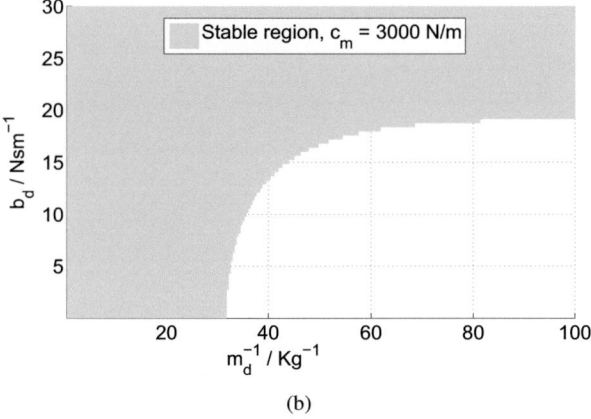

(b)

Fig. 6.7.: Stability boundaries of the semi-mobile haptic interface in the (m_d, b_d) parameter space for (a) high manipulator rigidity $c_m = 30000 \, \mathrm{Nm^{-1}}$, and for (b) low manipulator rigidity $c_m = 3000 \, \mathrm{Nm^{-1}}$.

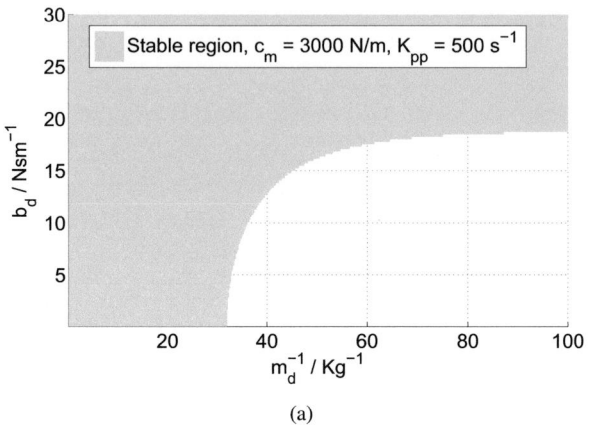

(a)

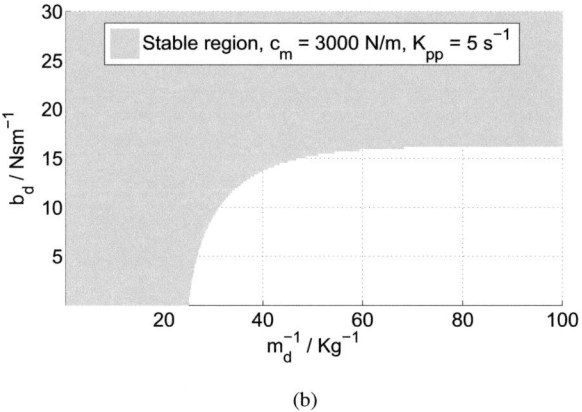

(b)

Fig. 6.8.: Stability boundaries of the semi-mobile haptic interface in the (m_d, b_d) parameter space with (a) high position gain of PPU $K_{pp} = 500\,\mathrm{s}^{-1}$, and with (b) low position gain of PPU $K_{pp} = 5\,\mathrm{s}^{-1}$.

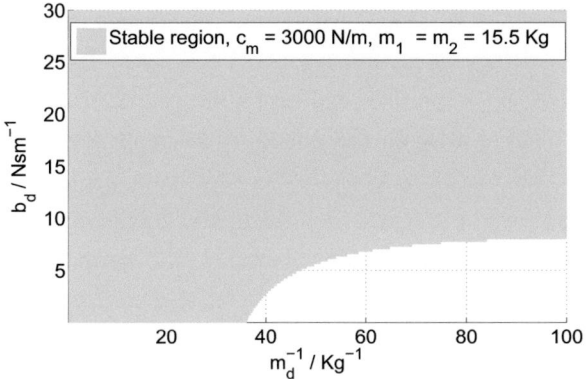

Fig. 6.9.: Stability boundaries of the semi-mobile haptic interface in the (m_d, b_d) parameter space for manipulator mass $m_1 = m_2 = 15.5 \, \text{kg}$.

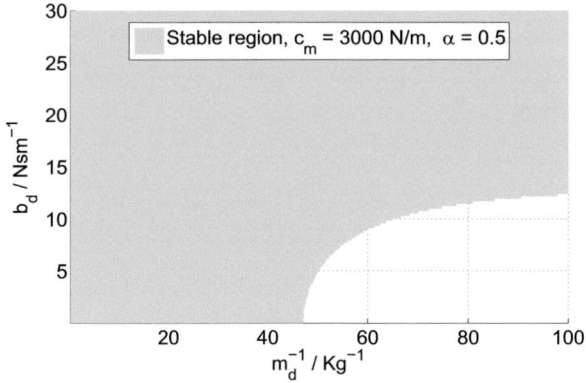

Fig. 6.10.: Stability boundaries of the semi-mobile haptic interface in the (m_d, b_d) parameter space for human compliance reduced by a factor $\alpha = 0.5$.

The control of the interface is based on the decoupling of wide-area motion control and force control, which is possible due to the planar redundant DOFs of semi-mobile haptic interfaces. A dedicated force control that makes use of a directional admittance model in order to shape the apparent dynamics of the haptic interface and render the guidance information was presented. In order to solve the redundancy of the haptic interface, and thus achieve wide-area motion, prepositioning algorithms for both setup configurations have been presented. For the frontal configuration, a prepositioning algorithm that considers the curvature of the user path significantly improves the utilization of the workspace in the user environment. The mirror configuration considerably simplifies the prepositioning algorithm, by positioning the PPU above the human operator and following his/her motions. Moreover, this prepositioning avoids fast motions of the PPU (due to fast motions of the user's hand) and permits the optimal utilization of the space in the user environment.

Finally, the effects of the dynamic properties of both subsystems, haptic manipulator and prepositioning unit, on the asymptotic stability of the admittance-controlled interface have been analyzed. For this purpose, the boundaries of the stable region in the parameter space given by the minimum desired target mass and damping were determined for variable dynamic parameters.

7. Realization of the New Semi-mobile Haptic Interface

Our first prototypical semi-mobile haptic interface with *frontal setup configuration* was described in [107, 145]. Fig. 7.1 shows this setup. Although this setup is principally suitable for extended range telepresence, some important drawbacks were asserted. On the one hand, the high weight, backlash, and inertia of the manipulator caused a poor force display quality in free space, since these effects cannot be completely compensated for by the force controller. On the other hand, the deficient utilization of the user environment and the difficult prepositioning of the PPU, which are intrinsic problems of the *frontal configuration* of the interface, as explained in Section 6.1, hindered to a great extent the experiments in wide-area telepresence scenarios.

In this chapter, the new design and the realization of a semi-mobile haptic interface with *mirror configuration* is presented in Section 7.1 and Section 7.2, respectively. The performance of the new haptic interface is systematically evaluated in Section 7.3, and finally, the whole system is experimentally evaluated, with navigation assistance for a virtual extended range scenario, in Section 7.4.

7.1. Mechanical Design

For the realization of the semi-mobile haptic interface with *mirror configuration*, a new haptic manipulator, which is attached to the Cartesian prepositioning unit (PPU), has been designed.

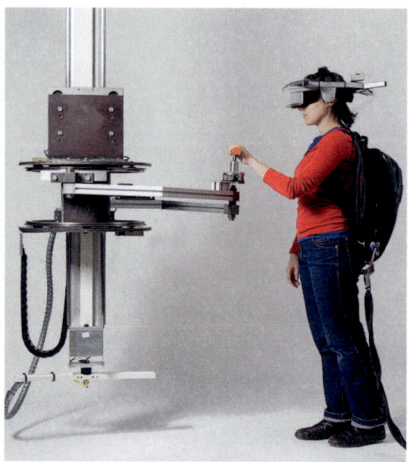

Fig. 7.1.: Prototype of the semi-mobile haptic interface with frontal setup configuration.

7.1.1. Requirements Specifications

The most important requirements for the new haptic manipulator can be summarized as follows:

- human-like output capability,

- human-like local workspace,

- good force display quality,

- and safe human-robot interaction.

A high output capability, i.e., the display of high forces and velocities in the range of those of humans, is essential for realistic haptic feedback. The haptic manipulator is thus designed to display forces up to 150 N, velocities up to 1 m/s, and accelerations up to 10 m/s^2 in the whole workspace. The force display quality has to be isotropic in the workspace, i.e., the quality of the force display is not direction-dependent. For this purpose, a force isotropy higher than 50% is needed inside the dexterous workspace.

The haptic manipulator for navigation assistance is designed to have a planar workspace, with two active DOFs and one passive rotational DOF. Therefore, the planar workspace of the manipulator has to cover the planar workspace of the human arm. The relevant workspace of the human arm, which is studied in [69], can be well approximated by a semicircle of radius 60 cm whose origin is situated at the right shoulder. A smaller semicircle with a radius of 25 cm centered at the human's position has to be removed from this workspace, which approximates the space occupied by the human body. The desired dexterous workspace of the manipulator is a hollow cylinder with external radius $r_e = 0.8$ m and internal radius $r_i = 0.25$ m.

In order to improve the force display quality in free space, the haptic manipulator has to be designed so as to have low inertia and zero backlash, since these effects limit the minimum inertia that can be displayed to the user, and thus limit the *transparency* of the force display as well. The mass of the manipulator must also be reduced in order to reduce the disturbing repositioning forces that arise when the PPU moves the manipulator. At the same time, the manipulator has to be very rigid so as to be able to realistically display hard contacts, because the rigidity of the haptic interface limits the maximum displayable rigidity. Finally, the measurement of the position of the end-effector must be measured exactly in order to achieve an accurate force display.

Safety is a major concern when designing robots that are in contact with humans. The mirror configuration of the manipulator considerably reduces the risk of injury through the crushing or trapping hazard caused by the moving prepositioning unit. However, the design has to guarantee that if a failure occurs, no danger for the user exists. The international standard ISO 10218, which regulates the safety requirements for industrial robots, considers a maximum static force of 150 N as tolerable. In service, the user activates the device with a dead man's switch, and robot safety functions of category 3 (ISO 13849-1) and stop category 0 or 1 (in accordance with IEC 60204) are required. Furthermore, areas with risk of a trapping hazard (e.g., at the limits of the user environment) are excluded from the workspace of the device.

For the kinematics of the manipulator, a parallel Selective Compliance Assembly Robot Arm (SCARA) with four links was selected because of its rigidity. Centrally driven joints at the base reduce the mass of the moving parts, increase the workspace (i.e., reduce the non-reachable region centered on the PPU), and allow infinite rotation around the vertical axis of the PPU.

7.1.2. Kinematic Design

Kinematic Equations

The kinematic model of the semi-mobile haptic interface is shown in Fig. 7.2. The PPU consists of two translational joints that locate the haptic manipulator at S_L. Two rotational joints situated at the base of the manipulator determine the end-effector pose S_E. The position of the end-effector can be expressed as explained in Section 6.3, by

$$\underline{x}_E = \underline{x}_L + \underline{x}_S \, . \tag{7.1}$$

Let us now consider the geometrical model of the manipulator arranged in a SCARA configuration as depicted in Fig. 7.3(b). L represents the position of the linear prepositioning unit, E the position of the end-effector, and l_1 and l_2 the lengths of the proximal and distal links, respectively. The angles α and β are actively driven, and the end-effector position $\underline{x}_E$ can be expressed as

$$\underline{x}_E = \begin{bmatrix} x_L \\ y_L \end{bmatrix} + \begin{bmatrix} \cos\left(\frac{\alpha+\beta}{2}\right) \cdot R \\ \sin\left(\frac{\alpha+\beta}{2}\right) \cdot R \end{bmatrix}, \tag{7.2}$$

where R, the radial distance from PPU is calculated as

$$R = l_1 \cos\left(\frac{\beta - \alpha}{2}\right) + \sqrt{l_2^2 - l_1^2 \sin^2\left(\frac{\beta - \alpha}{2}\right)} . \qquad (7.3)$$

The Jacobian of the manipulator $\mathbf{J}\left(\underline{\gamma}\right)$ on the configuration space $\underline{\gamma} = \begin{bmatrix} \alpha & \beta \end{bmatrix}^{\mathrm{T}}$ is defined as

$$\mathbf{J}\left(\underline{\gamma}\right) = \frac{\partial \underline{x}_S\left(\underline{\gamma}\right)}{\partial \underline{\gamma}} . \qquad (7.4)$$

The Jacobian maps a unit ball in the joint velocity space to an ellipsoid (manipulability ellipsoid) in the end-effector velocity space and depends on the actual joint configuration $\underline{\gamma}$. A manipulability measure based on the singular value decomposition of the Jacobian is now used to optimize the geometrical parameters of the manipulator l_1 and l_2.

Optimization of Global Manipulability Criterion

It has been well accepted that the most suitable local performance index is the condition number of the Jacobian [54], which represents the isotropy of the force output. Isotropy can be used to find the optimal configuration of a manipulator, i.e., the configuration at which the condition number of the Jacobian reaches its minimum value in the overall workspace. Furthermore, we can define a global index that permits us to optimize not only the configuration but also the geometry of the manipulator. For this purpose, first, a local *Conditioning Index* $\frac{1}{\kappa}$ is defined by

$$0 \leq \frac{1}{\kappa} = \frac{\sigma_2}{\sigma_1} \leq 1 , \qquad (7.5)$$

where κ is the condition number, and σ_2 and σ_1 are the minimum and maximum singular value of the Jacobian, respectively.

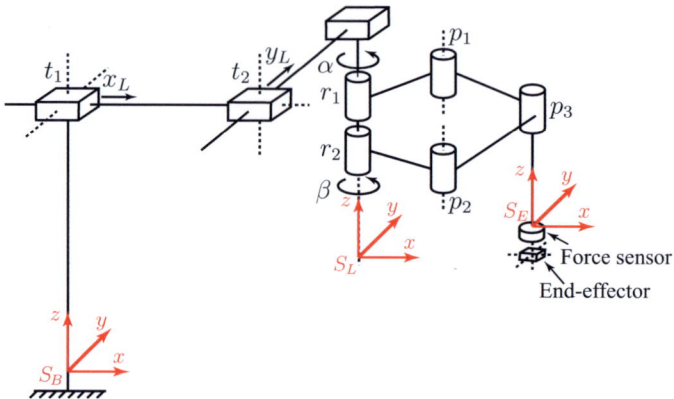

Fig. 7.2.: Kinematic model of the new semi-mobile haptic interface. Joints t_1 and t_2 locate the haptic manipulator at S_L (atop the user), joints r_1 and r_2 are actively driven and determine the end-effector pose at S_E, joints p_1, p_2, and p_3 are passive. This haptic interface is redundant in the planar degrees of freedom.

Let δ be the ratio of lengths of distal and proximal links, l_2 and l_1. δ has influence on the location, shape, and size of the workspace W_{k0}, which is bounded by a specific conditioning index $1/\kappa_0$, in our study $1/\kappa_0 = 0.5$.

The global index $1/\bar{\kappa}$, which represents the mean value of the conditioning index $1/\kappa$ in the workspace W_{k0}, must be maximized in order to find the optimal value of δ. In our implementation, $1/\bar{\kappa}$ can be numerically calculated by

$$1/\bar{\kappa}(\delta) = \frac{1}{M \times N} \sum_{M}^{m=1} \sum_{N}^{n=1} \frac{1}{\kappa_{mn}} , \qquad (7.6)$$

where $1/\kappa_{mn} \geq 1/\kappa_0$ is the value of $1/\kappa$ at the node $(m\,n)$ of the $(M-1) \times (N-1)$ equally meshed workspace $W_{k0}(\delta)$. As a result,

$$\delta^* = \arg\max_{\delta} \{1/\bar{\kappa}(\delta)\}. \qquad (7.7)$$

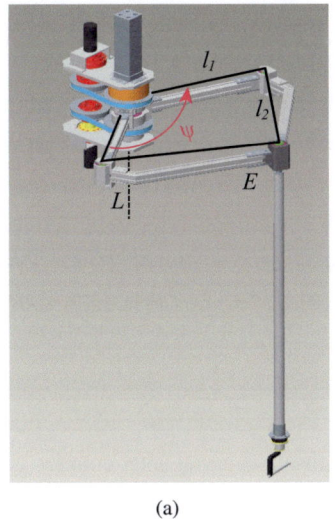

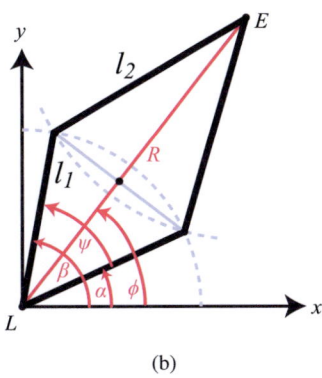

(a)   (b)

Fig. 7.3.: New manipulator design. (a) 3D-CAD Model of the haptic manipulator
as a Parallel Selective Compliance Assembly Robot Arm (SCARA) with
four links, two proximal links of length of l_1 and two distal links of length
l_2. (b) Geometrical model of the manipulator.

For the optimization, $l_2 > l_1$ was chosen because it produces a better-
shaped workspace for the given construction requirements. The result of
this optimization is $\delta^* = 1.2$. The other parameter restriction is defined
by the maximum distance of 1 m between the end-effector and the origin
of the end-effector, i.e., $l_1 + l_2 = 1$ m, which results in $l_1 = 0.45$ m and
$l_2 = 0.55$ m.

7.2. Setup

The haptic interface is built using commercially available components combined with self-designed aluminum construction elements. The actuation
torque of the rotational joints is provided by dc motors (Maxon RE40-40
150 W) coupled with harmonic drive gears (CPU-20-160-M) offering high

reduction (i=160) and zero backlash. The motors and the gears have been selected to meet the specifications described in Section 7.1.1.

The motor torque is transmitted to the links by toothed belts (reduction i=7/6) to permit a more compact design. The corresponding motor, power, and gear specification data can be found in Appendix A. The DC motors of the rotational joints are supplied by Copley amplifiers configured in torque mode. The joint angles are measured by optical encoders (HEDL5540-500imp, 3 channel) integrated in the wave, resulting in a very high resolution when multiplied by the gear ratio.

The haptic manipulator is equipped with the light six-axis force-torque sensor (Schunk FT-Mini-45) mounted at the end-effector, with a range of ± 290 N and accuracy of 0.25 N. A multi-channel slip contact ring (7K242F508) permits the unrestricted rotation around the vertical axis by providing for the electric transmission of the data of the force sensor and the state of the dead-man's switcher situated at the end-effector.

In order to protect the user and the system in the case of failure, mechanical safety couplings are mounted on the waves at the drives. The safety couplings disconnect the arms from the drives (i.e., they open the transmission chain) in case the motor torque exceeds a maximum permitted torque that is not reached in working conditions. The chosen couplings have a maximum switching torque up to 60 N, lower than the repeatable peak torque of the gears.

Fig. 7.3(a) shows the 3D-CAD model of the manipulator, and Fig. 7.4(a) shows its realization. The new design considerably reduces the mass and the inertia of the manipulator in comparison to the old prototype. The new manipulator weights $\approx$ 19 kg, and the mass of the moving parts is $\approx$ 7 kg. The new manipulator is attached to the linear PPU, which is realized as a grounded Cartesian robot of approximately 4×4 m^2. Each axis of the PPU consists of two parallel rails driven by synchronous AC motors. A magnetic measuring system mounted on the rails provides the position of the PPU with a resolution of 0.1 mm. Fig. 7.4(b) shows the setup of the whole semi-mobile haptic interface.

7.3. Performance Evaluation of the SMHI

7.3.1. Performance Measures of the SMHI

In [50, 91, 121], different performance measures and measurement procedures for the evaluation of haptic interfaces have been proposed. According to [91, 121], there are basically two types of performance measures: hardware-related performance measures and closed-loop performance measures.

Hardware-related measures depend on the hardware design of the haptic interface. The following all belong to these measures: the dexterous workspace (number of DOFs, and workspace free of singularities); the output capability (maximum peak and continuous force, maximum velocity, maximum acceleration, maximum payload); and the sensorial capability (measured quantities and resolution).

Closed-loop measures depend on the control law as well, and cannot be evaluated without assuming a certain force controller. These measures are force precision, force bandwidth, backdrivability, and apparent stiffness.

Environmental factors such as weight, utilization of the workspace, or operator safety are additional performance measures [50]. Although they are difficult to compare among different haptic interfaces, the new setup with the mirror setup configuration has managed to improve these factors when compared to the first prototype with the frontal setup configuration displayed in Fig. 7.1.

In order to reduce the number of experiments, a model-based performance evaluation [91, 121] is used to compute some of the performance measures. Other measures, however, can only be determined experimentally. In order to achieve repeatable measures, the user must be replaced, if possible, by a machine that simulates human grasping.

(a)

(b)

Fig. 7.4.: The new SMHI consisting of the prepositioning unit and the haptic manipulator.

7.3.2. Model-based Evaluation

Dexterous Workspace

The haptic manipulator has 2 active translational DOFs and 1 passive rotational DOF. The reachable workspace is the transversal section of a hollow cylinder with inner radius $r_{in} = l_2 - l_1 = 0.1$ m and outer radius $r_{out} = l_2 + l_1 = 1$ m. However the dexterous workspace of the manipulator excludes the regions in which the isotropy of the device (i.e., the inverse of the condition number) is $\frac{1}{\kappa} < 0.5$.

Fig. 7.5 displays the manipulability ellipsoids, the velocity manipulability [129], and the isotropy in the reachable workspace of the manipulator. The velocity manipulability, which represents the area of the ellipsoids, is particularly good between a radius 0.5 m and 0.8 m. The isotropy measure is given by the ratio of the axis of the manipulability ellipsoid. The closer the ellipsoids to the sphere, the more uniformly the haptic interface can move in different directions. The dexterous workspace chosen is the one in which the isotropy is higher than 0.5, which is described by a minimum radius $r_{min} = 0.25$ m and a maximum radius $r_{max} = 0.85$ m.

The form of the workspace of the manipulator, considerably simplifies the algorithm that takes care of the prepositioning of the manipulator. In fact, the optimal position of the manipulator is such that the center of the workspace coincides with the human position independently of the user's orientation. In this case, the coverage of the human's arm workspace is maximal.

Output Capability

The output capability in terms of maximum force, velocity, and acceleration determines the physical limits on interactions that can be performed with the device [121]. High force and acceleration capability are particularly important for the exploration of rigid objects in order to avoid penetration into immovable objects and to convincingly display hard contacts requiring

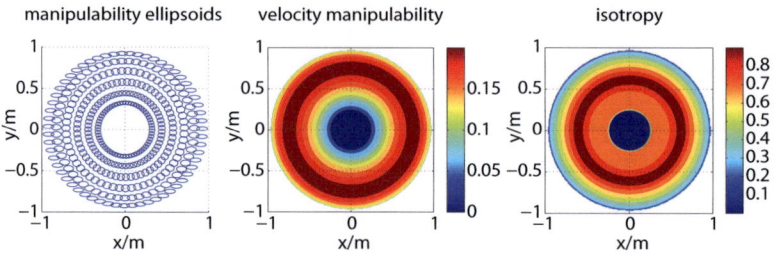

Fig. 7.5.: Manipulability ellipsoids (left), velocity manipulability (middle), and isotropy (right) in the reachable workspace of the manipulator.

rapid changes of velocity. A high velocity capability is needed for unconstrained motions involving high end-effector speeds. However, due to the device's nonlinearities, the maximum output capability typically varies significantly with the end-effector location and the direction of manipulation. A meaningful measure for the output performance is therefore the specification of the worst-case value of the output capability in the entire workspace.

The output capability of the device has been computed according to the algorithm presented in [121], which allows the analysis of the worst-case force/torque, velocity, and acceleration capability of the haptic manipulator. The computation of the output capability is based on the technical specifications of the motors and gears and on the following equations:

$$
\begin{aligned}
\underline{\dot{x}}_S &= \mathbf{J}\underline{\dot{\gamma}} \\
\underline{F} &= (\mathbf{J}^{-1})^T \underline{\tau} \,, \ \underline{\dot{\gamma}} = 0 \\
\underline{\ddot{x}}_S &= \mathbf{J}\hat{\mathbf{M}}_{\gamma}^{-1}\underline{\tau} \,, \ \underline{\dot{\gamma}}, \ \underline{F} = 0 \,,
\end{aligned}
\tag{7.8}
$$

where $\mathbf{J}$ is the Jacobian, which relates the joint velocities $\underline{\dot{\gamma}}$ to the Cartesian velocity $\underline{\dot{x}}_S$, and $\hat{\mathbf{M}}_{\gamma}$ is the mass matrix of the manipulator.

The hardware limitations on the output capability of the joints are given by the limit of the repeated torque and the maximum speed of the harmonic drive gears (cf. Appendix A), which is 107.3 Nm and 3.5 rad/s at the side of the arm (i.e., taking into consideration the reduction $i = 160 \times 7/6 = 187$).

The motor torques and joint velocities necessary to perform a constant force/velocity in the x-direction are calculated. The maximum allowed torques and joint velocities are then applied to produce the maximum force/velocity in the same direction at each point of the workspace. Fig. 7.6 shows the simulation results. Since the workspace is rotationally symmetric, the lowest achieved force, acceleration, and velocity are independent from the force/velocity direction. A commanded force/velocity in another direction would only result in the rotation of the diagrams displayed in Fig. 7.6.

By reducing the dexterous workspace to $r_{min} = 0.25$ m and $r_{max} = 0.85$ m, the minimum peak force capability is higher than 150 N, the minimum velocity is 1 m/s, and the minimum acceleration is 10 m/s^2 in the workspace, which correspond to the specifications.

The calculation of the continuous force capability is straightforward considering that the maximum continuous input torque due to hardware limitations of the motors (cf. Appendix A) is 34.3 Nm at the side of the arm. It is therefore obtained by multiplying the minimum peak force results by the factor $34.3/107.3$, which results in a worst continuous force of 48 N.

Sensorial Capability

The position resolution of the manipulator arm with the given encoders and the given reduction is $0.0077°$, which, assuming a maximum manipulator length of 1 m, results in a minimum position resolution of 0.13 mm at the end-effector. At the same time, the resolution of the system that measures the position of the PPU is 0.1 mm. The force sensor has a resolution of 0.25 N.

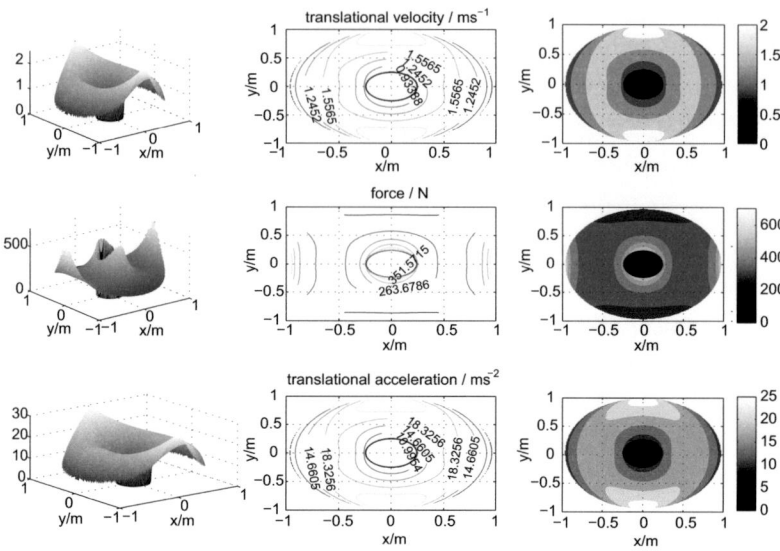

Fig. 7.6.: Maximum translational velocity, force, and acceleration capability.

Environmental Factors

The main improvement with respect to the old setup, besides the obvious safer operation, resides in the increase of the operating range seen by the user and a better utilization of the available space in the user environment. Fig. 7.7 and Fig. 7.8 illustrate these improvements. Since the workspace of the old setup has an outer radius $r_{max} = 0.90$ m and an inner radius $r_{min} = 0.50$ m, and since the user is outside the workspace of the manipulator, the operation range of the user for the current PPU configuration is reduced to a circle of radius $r = 0.20$ m. The new setup, however, permits the user to operate in the whole workspace of the manipulator from his/her current position.

At the same time, the area in which the user can walk in the user environment (the green area in Fig. 7.8) increases considerably with the new setup

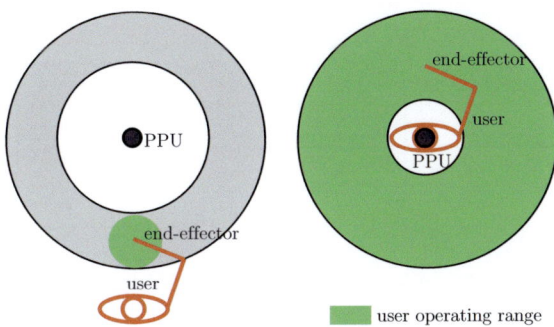

Fig. 7.7.: Operating range of the user at a certain position: with the old setup (left), and with the new setup (right).

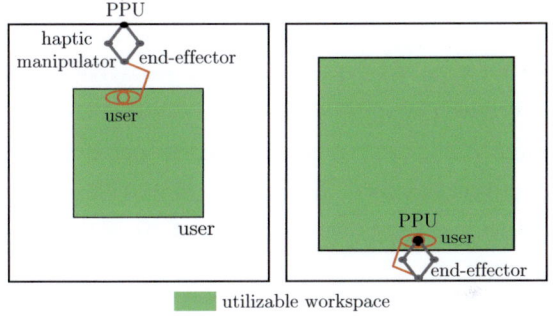

Fig. 7.8.: Utilizable area in the user environment: with the old setup (left), and with the new setup (right).

(from 20 % to the 60% of the total workspace), since the user can utilize nearly the whole workspace of the semi-mobile haptic interface.

The new setup reduces the mass of the manipulator by $\approx 75\%$ (from 80 kg to 19 kg), and the mass of the moving parts by $\approx 41\%$ (from 12 kg to 7 kg). The average inertia reduced at the motor wave for the new manipulator is $103 \cdot 10^{-6}$ kg m^2, which represents a reduction of $\approx 57\%$ compared to the old manipulator (with $238 \cdot 10^{-6}$ kg m^2).

Tab. 7.1.: Static Force Error

Target Force in x (N)	Target Force in y (N)	Mean Error in x (N)	Mean Error in y (N)
0	0	0.04	0.17
5	0	0.11	0.24
10	0	0.09	0.25
15	0	0.02	0.23
25	0	0.11	0.29
0	5	0.03	0.01
0	10	0.23	0.24
0	15	0.00	0.08
0	25	0.22	0.30
10	10	0.26	0.14

7.3.3. Measured-based Evaluation

The closed-loop performance measures depend on the control of the haptic interface. They are also called transparency measures because they quantify the difference between the given system and a *perfect transparent* system, in which the human is in direct contact with the target environment. Except when other values are specified, the standard control parameters used in this evaluation in both x and y directions are $K_p = 60$, $K_d = 15.5$, $m_d = 5$ kg, and $b_d = 10$ Nsm^{-1}.

Force Precision

Static force fidelity was identified under isometric conditions by attaching the end-effector of the haptic manipulator to a fixed position. Because the firm grasp reduces the stability of the haptic device (as explained in Section 6.6), the control gains had to be reduced ($K_p = 10$, $K_d = 6.3$). The mean absolute force error for different values of the reference force in the orthogonal directions x and y is displayed in Table 7.1. As expected, under admittance control, due to the integral action of the inner control loop, the static force error virtually corresponds to the resolution of the force sensor of 0.25 N.

The dynamic force precision describes the performance of the force controller to track dynamically changing force commands while the device end-effector is held stationary. A high force bandwidth is necessary to provide a crisp sensation during hard contacts in which all frequencies are present. The force bandwidth of the system was experimentally determined under isometric conditions using a sinus-shaped signal with varying frequency and amplitude 20 N as the input reference force.

Because the stiffness of the required coupling by far exceeds the stiffness of a human arm, the control gains and the desired inertia had to be significantly reduced to maintain stability ($K_p = 10$, $K_d = 6.3$, $m_d = 60$ kg, and $b_d = 30$ Nsm^{-1}). However, the reduction of the control gain is associated with a decrease of the closed loop performance [121]. In fact, the resulting bandwidth of the system under these conditions was very low, about 3 Hz. This small force bandwidth was in part a result of the high assumed mass m_d, and of the limited rigidity of the control under these conditions, so that the force bandwidth of the system when the human grasps the end-effector (i.e. when the desired mass can be reduced and the control gains can be increased) is expected to be higher.

Backdrivability

In admittance control, the qualitative description of backdrivability corresponds to the fidelity of the displayed admittance in terms of target mass and damping. This is usually very accurate under motion inputs with moderate bandwidth due to the high gain of the inner control loop closed on motion, which effectively compensates for disturbance forces due to the device dynamics.

Experiments were performed to investigate the impedance fidelity. In all experiments, the test persons have been asked to try very hard to excite all

Tab. 7.2.: Mass and Damping Fidelity

Target Impedance		Identified Impedance		Fidelity Factor	
m_t (Kg)	b_t (Ns/m)	m_i (Kg)	b_i (Ns/m)	f_m	f_b
5	15	4.58	13.98	0.91	0.93
5	10	4.77	8.77	0.95	0.87
10	10	9.58	8.38	0.95	0.83
15	10	13.01	8.21	0.87	0.82
15	15	12.99	13.88	0.86	0.92
15	30	13.82	27.88	0.92	0.93
30	5	24.01	3.13	0.80	0.63
10	50	9.13	48.01	0.91	0.96
10	100	8.22	96.16	0.82	0.96
10	150	6.31	142.51	0.63	0.95
10	200	5.33	179.84	0.53	0.89

frequencies of the device. Analog to [91], a fidelity factor is calculated for mass and damping. The mass fidelity factor is defined as

$$f_m = 1 - \frac{|m_t - m_i|}{m_t}, \tag{7.9}$$

where m_t means target mass and m_i identified mass. An analog factor is defined for damping f_b. The experimental results for several commanded impedances are displayed in Table 7.2.

Another convenient measure for the backdrivability of haptic interfaces operated in the admittance display mode seems to be the specification of the minimum inertia that can be commanded without producing instability at arbitrarily interactions performed by a human operator [121]. As shown in Section 6.6, the stability bound for the target mass depends on the virtual damping. In all the experiments described below the test persons have been asked to try very hard to produce instability with end-effector motions at varying grip strengths. The minimum displayable inertia using the standard control gains is displayed for different damping conditions in Fig. 7.9. The minimum inertia at zero damping is $m_d = 4$ kg. This inertia could be reduced by increasing damping until $m_d = 2$ kg at damping $b_d = 80$ Nsm^{-1}.

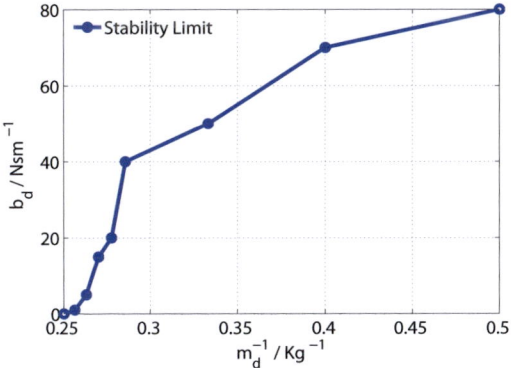

Fig. 7.9.: Experimentally identified limit of stability region of the admittance-controlled semi-mobile haptic interface.

Stiffness

The stiffness of the force-controlled manipulator can be evaluated by simulating a wall with the desired stiffness k_t and letting the test persons push against this virtual wall. On the basis of the measured displacement of the end-effector and the measured force, the apparent stiffness of the wall can be approximated. The experimentally identified control stiffness k_c is displayed in Fig. 7.10.

For an exact measure of the maximum stiffness, it is not the position seen from the motor encoders that should be considered, but rather the actual endpoint position, including all sources of mechanical device elasticity [121]. However, this position is usually not available. Therefore, when the control law does not explicitly consider the elasticity of the manipulator, the apparent stiffness k_D is given by the serial connection of the control stiffness k_c (seen from the motor encoders) and the mechanical stiffness k_m as

$$k_D = k_c \frac{k_m}{k_c + k_m} \ .$$

(7.10)

143

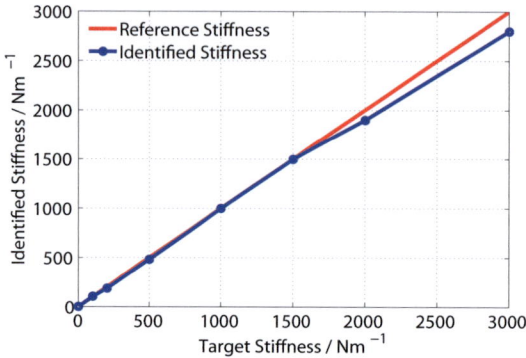

Fig. 7.10.: Experimentally identified stiffness of the admittance-controlled semi-
mobile haptic interface.

Although a detailed evaluation of the old setup is beyond the scope of
this work, an experimental comparison between both setups [51] showed
that the impedance fidelity — i.e., the backdrivability and stiffness fidelity,
and therefore the *transparency* of the force display — is much higher with
the new setup. The increased force display quality is mainly due to the
improved mechanical lightweight mechanical design with lower inertia and
almost zero backlash.

7.4. Performance Evaluation of the Overall System

Real experiments have been performed in order to demonstrate the feasibil-
ity and evaluate the benefits of the whole system for navigation assistance
in an extended-range telepresence scenario.

7.4.1. Method

Scenario

A virtual telepresence task that consists in finding and dismantling bombs
in an extensive target environment is chosen. A bird's eye view and an ego

(a)   (b)

Fig. 7.11.: Screen shots of the virtual scenario for dismantling bombs.

view of the scenario are displayed in Fig. 7.11. From the ego view, the position of the hand is represented by a white ball. The task consists in two subtasks: first, accurately following a predefined path; and second, reaching two bombs whose positions are unknown to the human operator. The length of the path is 15 m and the ground floor of the building is 25×15 m².

The human performance is compared with regard to three haptic conditions: a) without any haptic information, which will be called *visual* (V) for the sake of simplicity; b) with haptic contact information, or *walls* (W) for short; and c) with haptic guidance information, or *guidance* (G) for short.

Performance Measures

The following performance measures have been considered: the *execution time* of each subtask; the *covered distance* in each subtask; and either the *path deviation* for the path-directed task or the *collision error* for the goal-directed task.

The *execution time* T describes the period spanning from the start of the subtask at a time t_s and the end of the subtask at time t_e as

$$T = t_e - t_s .$$

(7.11)

Another important measure for task performance is the *covered distance* S when performing a navigation task. The smaller S is, the more efficiently the task has been carried out. This measure is determined by calculating the Euclidean norm of the vector difference $\Delta \underline{x} = [\Delta x, \Delta y]$ of two consecutive measured positions and summing these up over a certain time period given by n steps

$$S = \sum_{i=1}^{n} \|\Delta \underline{x}_i\| \ . \tag{7.12}$$

The *path deviation* D_P for the path-directed task is defined as the mean absolute value of the distance to the desired path (i.e., the Euclidean distance to the nearest point on the path $\underline{x}_p$)

$$D_P = \frac{1}{n} \sum_{i=1}^{n} \|\underline{x}_i - \underline{x}_p\| \ . \tag{7.13}$$

The *collision error* D_O is calculated as the integral of the penetration depth Δp into the obstacles over the time in which this penetration occurs

$$D_O = \frac{1}{F} \sum_{i=1}^{n} \|\Delta p_i\| \ , \tag{7.14}$$

where F is the frequency of the measurements, i.e., the number of steps per second.

In order to measure the subjective workload of the participants, a self-reported workload assessment captured by the NASA Task Load Index (NASA-TLX) [47] was used. This questionnaire, together with the used demographic questionnaire, is found in Appendix B.

Experimental Setup and Guidance Implementation

The operator holds the end-effector of the haptic manipulator presented in Section 7.2 while carrying the user interface displayed in Fig. 7.12, which

Fig. 7.12.: Human system interface of extended range telepresence system.

consists of a head-mounted-display and a wearable unit [143], which serves to track the operator position and to visualize the target environment.

The optimal region of the prepositioning algorithm of the semi-mobile haptic interface (which is described in Section 6.5.2) is defined by $R^*_{min} = 0.43$ m and $R^*_{max} = 0.67$ m. The scaling factors of the mapping between the positions of the prepositioning unit and the human operator are $S_{in} = 1$ and $S_{out} = 0.8$.

Path-directed guidance was realized as combined guidance, implemented as a constant active force along the preferred direction $F_G = 8$ N and a passive component with $D_\perp = 300$ Ns/m. Goal-directed guidance was implemented as passive guidance with $D_\perp = 300$ Ns/m. The calculation of the PHGF for both simultaneous targets allows the operator to choose the order in which he/she reaches them.

147

Experimental Design and Participants

The procedure included: (1) completing a demographic questionnaire; (2) a briefing on the telepresence scenario and instructions about how to use the telepresence system; and (3) familiarization with the haptic interface and the feeling of virtual walls through a short practice trial. Afterwards, the evaluation trials for the given scenario were performed, and these had to be conducted successively under the three haptic conditions presented above: *visual* (V), *walls* (W), and *guidance* (G).

In each trial, participants were instructed to complete both sequential subtasks as quickly and as accurately as possible: the first subtask was to follow the blue path; and the second was to find and reach (deactivate) two targets (bombs) in the order they prefer.

To prevent the participants from learning the positions of the targets (bombs) in advance, these positions were systematically varied in each trial in such a way that the minimum covered distance required to find both targets was always the same.

At the end of each trial, participants were asked to provide ratings of five workload factors and answer some questions about the feeling of presence in the telepresence system.

A total of 12 subjects between 23 and 44 years old (the mean age was 27.67 years, and the standard deviation 5.97 years) participated in this experiment. There were 2 women among the participants, 9 right-handed people, and 5 people without prior experience with the telepresence system. The average time spent playing 3D-computer games by the participants was stated to be 6.08 hours per month (the standard deviation was 8.60).

7.4.2. Results

The mean and the standard deviation of the performance measures for the path-directed and the goal-directed subtasks are shown in Fig. 7.13 and Fig. 7.14. An analysis of variance (ANOVA) was conducted to investigate the influence of the feedback modality in the performance measures. To understand the differences in performance that result from the modalities, (Tukey-Kramer adjusted) multiple comparison tests were also performed.

Execution Time: Regarding the path-directed subtask, the repeated measures ANOVA revealed significant differences ($p < 0.05$) between the execution times of the different modalities. The multiple comparison tests between modalities revealed that the haptic modality without guidance (*walls* (W)) is outperformed by the other modalities (*visual* (V) and *guidance* (G)). However, no significant difference has been found between *visual* and *guidance* modality.

The smallest mean execution time for the second task (goal-directed task) is achieved for the *guidance* (G) modality. However, a significant difference was only found with respect to the *walls* modality.

Covered Path: The shortest covered path was achieved by the *visual* modality, and this was significantly shorter than the covered path for the *walls* and *guidance* modalities. Although the covered path in the goal-oriented task is shorter for the *guidance* modality, significant differences ($p < 0.05$) could not be found among the different modalities.

Deviation / Collision Error: The smallest mean deviation from the desired path in the path-directed task is achieved with the *guidance* modality. However, the repeated measures ANOVA only revealed a significant difference with respect to the *walls* modality.

Only 2 out of 12 participants had collisions with the virtual obstacles during the experiments performed with the *guidance* modality, compared to 5 participants within the *walls* modality, and 6 participants within the *visual* modality. The collision error, which is the integral of the penetration depth over the time, shows a great variability within subjects, however, so that no significant differences among conditions could be identified.

Workload: Fig. 7.14 shows the results for the performance measure workload, which was evaluated using the NASA-TXL questionnaire. The plots reveal a smaller workload with the *guidance* condition. However, the

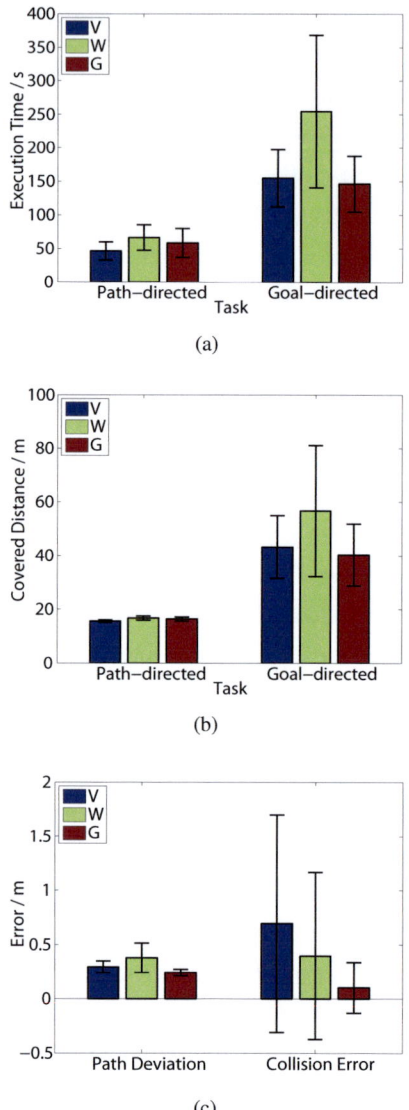

(a)

(b)

(c)

Fig. 7.13.: Mean and standard deviation of performance measures in both subtasks (the path-directed subtask and the goal-directed subtask) for three haptic modalities (*visual* (V), *walls* (W), and *guidance* (G)).

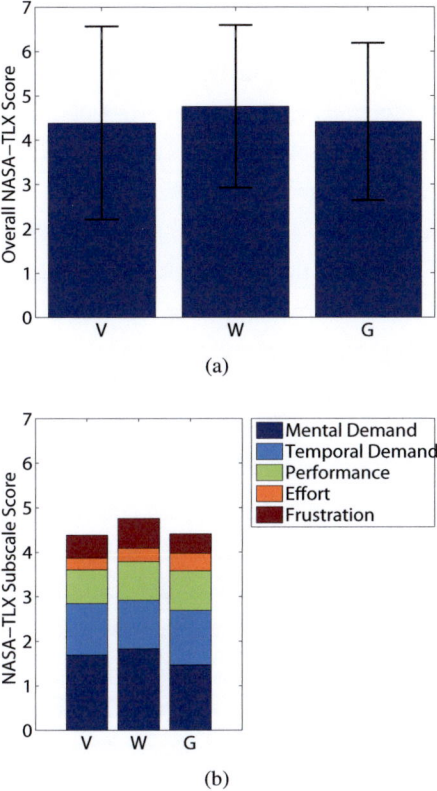

Fig. 7.14.: Mean and standard deviation of workload measure for the whole task. (a) Overall NASA-TXL score for the *visual* (V), *walls* (W), and *guidance* (G) modalities. (b) NASA-TLX subscale score for the three modalities.

difference is not significant when compared to the other conditions using the repeated ANOVA.

When looking at the contribution of each factor to the overall workload, it becomes clear that the *guidance* modality reduces the mental workload and the frustration of participants; however, it also increases the effort the participants exert in comparison to the other modalities.

7.4.3. Discussion

The experimental evaluation of the system with haptic guidance suggests that the assistance functions lead to an improvement in performance, but only compared to the haptic telepresence system without guidance.

The shorter completion time and covered distance in the path-directed task with visual feedback is achieved, to some extent, at the expense of accuracy, since the mean of the path deviation with guidance tends to be smaller. On the other hand, in order to overcome the limited field of view of the head-mounted display, the desired path was drawn at the waist-height, which results in an additional visual assistance.

A greater difference was expected in the execution time of the goal-oriented task. A possible reason for this small difference may result from the simplicity of the goal-directed task. In fact, at the beginning of the goal-directed task, the user has to choose one of two equally probable directions (left or right). Once the user has chosen the correct direction, finding the targets is quite straightforward, as they can eventually be seen from the corridor (from the right positions).

It is interesting that the modality with haptic feedback without guidance (the *wall* condition) results in a greater covered distance in the goal-directed task. We observed that participants were prone to miss the targets even when they walked past them, and that they then had to turn around to find them. Our hypothesis is that this may occur because participants feel more restricted in their motions when they are attached to the haptic interface than they do without the haptic interface.

Haptic guidance considerably reduces collisions with obstacles, but it does not eliminate collisions entirely. A further increase in the level of guidance could potentially reduce this, but this would also increase the human effort involved, which was already reported to be higher compared to the other conditions. These results confirm the necessity of adapting the guidance level online to suit the current user's need.

According to the workload measures, haptic guidance succeeds in reducing the mental demand of the participants. However, the high variability of the measures within subjects makes it difficult to find statistically significant differences among the conditions.

Finally, it is important to note, that even after a short familiarization run, every single participant was able to complete the task, which demonstrates the system's excellent usability. However, the highest workload value of the *wall* condition suggests that it makes it more complicated for users to operate the haptic system with the semi-mobile haptic interface, although haptic guidance helps to reduce this workload and improve thus task performance.

7.5. Summary

In this chapter, the new design and the prototypical realization of a semi-mobile haptic interface with *mirror setup configuration* have been presented. The main benefits of the new design are the safer operation and the higher maneuverability of the interface. In addition, the lighter and more compact design allowed for an improvement of the haptic device's force display quality compared to the previous setup.

The performance of the semi-mobile haptic interface has been evaluated using both model-based methods (in order to identify the output capability of the interface) and experimental methods (in order to determine the closed-loop performance measures). Finally, the performance of the whole telepresence system with haptic guidance has been experimentally evaluated using a virtual extended-range telepresence scenario. The experiments verified that, in comparison to the haptic telepresence system without haptic guidance, haptic guidance succeeds in reducing the mental workload of participants during the task, in reducing the collision with obstacles, and in improving the accuracy of the path-directed task.

8. Summary, Conclusions, and Future Work

The goal of this thesis has been the development of haptic navigation assistance for extended range telepresence systems. The objective of this assistance is to support the human operator in both the target and the user environment while making the telepresence system more intuitive. In this chapter, the results of this research and suggestions for future research directions are summarized.

The motivation for navigation assistance in extended range telepresence arises from the necessity of making telepresence systems more intuitive and easier to operate. On the one hand, real telepresence systems are affected by limitations such as reduced field of view, time delays, kinematic restrictions of teleoperators, etc., which complicate the navigation in the target environment. On the other hand, the navigation assistance aims to increase task performance, e.g., by increasing motion accuracy and reducing execution time, while reducing the workload of the operator.

The underlying idea of the navigation assistance is to combine the particular strengths of the human operator (decision making, the possibility of reacting to unforeseen events, prioritizing objectives, etc.) and the strengths of the robotic teleoperator (e.g., resistance to adverse environmental conditions, working accuracy). For this reason, it is essential for the haptic assistance not to interfere with the plans of the operator, but instead to support him/her in carrying out his/her plans. Extended range telepresence presents a further challenge, since the user has to be guided in an arbitrarily large target environment with haptic cues applied in the restricted user environment.

8.1. Summary and Results

In Chapter 2, a classification of existing assistance paradigms was presented. The haptic assistance presented in this work can be embedded in the paradigm of *virtual fixtures*, which provide the highest level of user control, since the teleoperator precisely follows the motion of the operator. Most existing literature about haptic assistance is basically concerned with telepresent or cooperative manipulation systems, which all assume a static user. In these systems, the user's hand motion is controlled to follow a given trajectory, which is the same in both the user and the target environment. In addition, most assistance functions depend on exact task information, so that the guidance in a modified environment or towards new goals would require the laborious task of generating and training new models.

Chapter 3 presents the concept of novel navigation assistance, which relies only on the location of the intended goals and obstacles. In order to assist the user in navigating towards his/her desired goal in an intuitive way, two human navigation models are considered depending on the current task: *path-directed* and *goal-directed* navigation. In *path-directed* navigation, the human is guided along a previously calculated desired path towards the goal; whereas in *goal-directed* navigation the guidance calculates, at each time step, the new optimal path that leads to the current desired goal by avoiding the obstacles. The benefit of this navigation assistance is that it does not rely on a fixed path, but is instead actualized dynamically.

In order to provide the user with consistent visual and haptic information in arbitrarily large target environments, the inferred optimal path is transformed with Motion Compression into a path which fits into the user environment. The resulting mapping between target and user environment is then used to transform the pose of the user into the target environment and the haptic information back into the user environment.

Chapter 4 presents a guidance function, the Plenhaptic Guidance Function (PHGF), for each of these navigation models. The particularity of the

PHGF is that it provides information not only about the desired direction of motion, but also about the required guidance in the other directions. In addition, the formalism of the PHGF allows for the guidance information towards simultaneous (or equally probable) goals to be specified.

The transformation of the guidance information into haptic commands (i.e., the rendering of the PHGF) is performed using two different force control methods. A kinematic model of the user as an underactuated system is used to derive the haptic commands, which when applied on the user's hand assist him in walking along the desired direction of motion. The *active* force control method guides the user by means of external forces applied to his/her hand. With *active* force control method, it is possible to achieve temporal guidance (i.e., the user can be guided towards a desired position at a given time) and also to regulate the posture of the user (i.e., control his/her position and his/her orientation). The *passive* force control method reorients the force applied by the user towards the desired direction of motion. The main benefit of this force control method is that if the user walks in the desired direction, no haptic corrections have to be applied, which results in a more transparent telepresence experience. However, no temporal guidance can be achieved and the final orientation of the operator cannot be directly controlled.

The effect of the strength of the guidance on the user's navigation performance is experimentally analyzed in Chapter 5. The main finding of the user study was that the best performance (in terms of lowest execution time, highest accuracy, and lowest human effort) is achieved by the combination of *active* and *passive* force control methods. Guidelines for adjusting the assistance level based on the gathered experimental data were also given.

One of the main challenges in the realization of the telepresence system with haptic navigation assistance is the development of a haptic interface that is capable of displaying both interaction forces and guidance commands in the whole user environment. Semi-mobile haptic interfaces, which consist of a prepositioning unit and a haptic manipulator, have proven to be particularly well suited for haptic extended range telepresence. In Chapter 6, a new semi-mobile haptic interface with *mirror setup config-uration* is presented. This configuration, in which the prepositioning unit is above the user, considerably simplifies the prepositioning algorithm to decouple the motion of the prepositioning unit and the haptic manipulator. As a result, better coverage of the user's arm workspace, better utilization of the available space in the user environment, and safer operation of the interface are achieved.

The effects of the dynamic properties of the subsystems of the semi-mobile haptic interface on asymptotic stability of the admittance-controlled interface have been analyzed. An important finding was that the stability of the interface does not depend on the dynamic properties of the prepositioning unit if this is very rigid, as is generally the case. On the one hand, a more flexible haptic manipulator leads to a more stable system, i.e., to a smaller amount of minimum inertia that can be displayed in free motion, but it does so at the cost of reducing the displayed rigidity of hard contacts. On the other hand, the more rigid the grip of the user, the more instable the admittance-controlled haptic interface becomes.

The prototypical realization of the semi-mobile haptic interface with *mirror configuration* is presented in Chapter 7. The haptic manipulator's lightweight and compact design allowed for an increase in the force display accuracy compared to the previous prototype. The performance of the new haptic manipulator was proven to meet the required specifications us-ing both model-based and experimental methods. Finally, the whole haptic telepresence system with haptic navigation assistance was experimentally evaluated in a virtual demining task in a very large target scenario. The experiments revealed that the system with haptic assistance succeeds in re-ducing the mental demand of participants and increasing task performance compared to the haptic telepresence system without assistance.

8.2. Conclusions

The main benefits of the developed haptic guidance system are:

- The haptic guidance system does not rely on explicit instructions or prior plans. Instead, the optimal path that leads to the current intended goal and that helps the user avoid the obstacles is inferred from the current user position and context information from the target environment. According to two different human navigation models, the user is then guided by means of haptic cues applied to his/her hand either to the originally predicted path (with *path-directed guidance*) or towards the intended goal (with *goal-directed guidance*) by updating the optimal path from the current user position online. As a result, the user can change both the goal and the desired path on the fly.

- This is the first system that provides haptic assistance in arbitrarily large target environments, which is achieved by combining the haptic guidance concept with Motion Compression. To achieve consistent haptic and visual guidance, the current inferred path is transformed with Motion Compression into a path that fits into the user environment. If goal-directed guidance is used, the calculation and the transformation of this path are performed dynamically at each time step. The same nonlinear mapping between the user and the target environment linearized at the current user position is used to transform the guidance haptic commands back into the user environment. This concept for wide-area haptic assistance can be employed with other types of guidance cues and can be applied to other tasks that are different from these navigation tasks.

- The novel SMHI with *mirror setup configuration* simultaneously increases the maneuverability of the haptic interface and achieves a safer operation by prepositioning the manipulator in such a way that the basis of the manipulator, the prepositioning unit, coincides with the user's position. This design can be used with haptic manipulators with more DOFs. Using, for example, a haptic manipulator with 6 DOF like the one presented in [91], in which angular and translational DOFs are decoupled, the *mirror setup configuration* could be realized by placing the translational DOFs on top of the user and the angular DOFs (the wrist) at the height of the user's hand.

Although this assistive telepresence system has been evaluated using only virtual target environments, the application to real target environments is (without taking into account non-ideal network conditions and technical implementation issues) straightforward. For the application of the proposed haptic guidance to real target environments the position of the teleoperator in the target environment has to be known. The localization of the teleoperator outdoors can be achieved via GPS. Instead, the localization of the teleoperator indoors has to be gained via odometry in combination with proximity exteroceptive sensors (like a laser range finder) and a map of the building, either given in advance or built by the teleoperator itself during the motion. It is then possible to correct the estimate provided by the odometry by comparing the expected measures of the exteroceptive sensors with the actual readings [114].

The necessity of haptic guidance in arbitrarily large target environments arises in many practical applications, for instance: applications that require the use of human navigation and decision capabilities (e.g., exploration and reconnaissance of remote areas); applications with challenging scenarios, in which the teleoperator can be damaged and/or there are bad visibility conditions for the operator (e.g., rescue missions, cleaning of contaminated areas); and in virtual or real scenarios, in which the operator is encouraged to reach certain areas of interest (e.g., tele-shopping, tele-sightseeing) and to avoid certain regions (e.g., training of evacuations).

8.3. Outlook for Future Work

On the basis of this work, several future directions of research appear —
whether they are direct extensions of the presented algorithms, or funda-
mentally new applications of the presented concepts.

Within the Plenhaptic Guidance Function (PHGF), further integration of
context information is conceivable. For example, for a predictive calculation of the PHGF, explicit consideration could be given to models of dynamic obstacles, to uncertainties in the position of the teleoperator, and also
to time-delays. In addition, the online adaptation of the level of guidance,
based either on the current (or estimated future) task performance or on the
force applied by the user as a measure of agreement or disagreement [87],
would reduce human effort and make the system more effective.

The effects of Motion Compression on human navigation could also be
considered in haptic assistance in order to compensate for them. Although
the limits of the user environment are implicitly considered in the navigation assistance through the path transformation performed by the Motion
Compression, these limits could be explicitly considered in order to restrict
the motion of the user towards them.

In this work, we assumed a bilateral telepresence system in which the
robot precisely follows the motion of the user. However, as many efforts try
to endow robots with more intelligence and autonomy, a telepresence system with sliding autonomy in which the teleoperator semi-autonomously
performs some simple tasks could permit a single operator to take care of
several teleoperators at the same time, and thus realize more complex tasks
in the target environment. On the other hand, the extension to multiple users
is also a predominant research direction in telepresence. For this purpose,
the intentions of all operators must be estimated and fused into a common
motion plan.

Finally, the proposed navigation assistance could be applied to other
types of haptic interfaces, e.g., to wearable haptic interfaces, and is not

restricted to telepresence systems, but can also be directly applied to collaborative navigation systems in which the target environment coincides with the user environment. In any case, the ground for further research has been prepared.

A. Setup Specifications

Joints	Gears				Motor			
	Series-Size-Ratio	MR [Nm]	MA [Nm]	vmax [rpm]	Type	Mh [Nm]	Mc [Nm]	vmax [rpm]
1, 2	CPU-20-160-M	92	49	6500	RE40 148867	2.28	0.17	7580

Encoders		Power Amplifier	Slip Ring	Safety Clutches	
Type	I [imp./r]	Type	Type	Type	Max. Torque [Nm]
HEDL5540	500	Copley 4122CE	7k-242-F	SKI/60/F/13/55/50-60	55

FT-Sensor			
Type	Calibration	Resolution [N]	Mass [g]
FTD-Mini45-R-2.5	SI-290-10-322061	0.2	90

MR: limit for repeated torque
MA: limit for average torque
vmax: maximum input speed
Mh: stall torque
Mc: maximum continuous torque
I: impulses per turn

Fig. A.1.: Hardware specifications of mechanical components of haptic manipulator.

B. Demographic and Workload Questionnaires

B. Demographic and Workload Questionnaires

Demographic Questionnaire

Last name:_____   First name:_____

Age: _____   Sex: Female:__   Male:__

Handedness: Right-handed:__   Left-handed:__

Are you experienced with 3D-computer games: very much__   much__   average__   little__   not at all__

Total amount of hours per month with 3D-computer games: _____

Are you experienced with the system at ISAS: very much__   much__   average__   little__   not at all__

NASA-TLX Mental Workload Rating Scale
FEEDBACK MODALITY:

Please place an "X" along each scale at the point that best indicates your experience with the display configuration.

Mental Demand: How much mental and perceptual activity was required (e.g., thinking, deciding, calculating, remembering, looking, searching, etc.)?

Low   High

Temporal Demand: How much time pressure did you feel due to the rate or pace at which the tasks or task elements occurred?

Low   High

Performance: How successful do you think you were in accomplishing the goals of the task set by the experimenter (or yourself)? How satisfied were you with your performance in accomplishing these goals?

Good   Poor

Effort: How hard did you have to work (mentally and physically) to accomplish your level of performance?

Low   High

Frustration: How insecure, discouraged, irritated, stressed and annoyed versus secure, gratified, content, relaxed and complacent did you feel during the task?

Low   High

Do not write below this line. Experimenter use only.
Subject #: _____   Trial No.:

166

List of Figures

List of Tables

Bibliography

[1] D. Aarno, S. Ekvall, and D. Kragić. Adaptive Virtual Fixtures for Machine–Assisted Teleoperation Tasks. In *IEEE International Conference on Robotics and Automation*, pages 1151–1156, 2005.

[2] J. J. Abbott. *Virtual Fixtures for Bilateral Telemanipulation*. PhD thesis, The Johns Hopkins University, 2005.

[3] J. J. Abbott. Pseudo-admittance Bilateral Telemanipulation with Guidance Virtual Fixtures. In *Proceedings of the IEEE Symposium on Haptic Interfaces for Virtual Environment and Teleoperator Systems*, 2006.

[4] J. J. Abbott, P. Marayong, and A. M. Okamura. Haptic Virtual Fixtures for Robot-Assisted Manipulation. In *Proceedings of the 12th International Symposium of Robotics Research*, pages 49–64, 2005.

[5] J. J. Abbott and A. M. Okamura. Analysis of Virtual Fixture Contact Stability for Teleoperation. In *Proceedings of the IEEE/RSJ International Conference on Intelligent Robots and Systems*, pages 2699–2706, 2003.

[6] J. J. Abbott and A. M. Okamura. Stable Forbidden-Region Virtual Fixtures for Bilateral Telemanipulation. *Journal of Dynamic Systems, Measurement, and Control*, 128:53–64, 2006.

[7] R. J. Adams and B. Hannaford. Stable Haptic Interaction with Virtual Environments. *IEEE Transactions on Robotics and Automation*, 15(3):465–474, 1999.

[8] P. Aigner and B. McCarragher. Human Integration into Robot Control Utilising Potential Fields. In *Proceedings of the IEEE International Conference on Robotics and Automation*, pages 291–296, 1997.

[9] P. Arcara and C. Melchiorri. Control Schemes for Teleoperation with Time Delay: A Comparative Study. *Robotics and Autonomous Systems*, 38(1):49–64, 2002.

[10] R. N. Banavar and V. Sankaranarayanan. *Switched Finite Time Control of A Class of Underactuated Systems*. Lecture Notes in Control And Information Sciences. Springer, 2006.

[11] F. Barbagli, A. Formaglio, M. Franzini, A. Giannitrapani, and D. Prattichizzo. *Experimental Robotics IX*, chapter An Experimental Study of the Limitations of Mobile Haptic Interfaces. STAR (Springer Tracts on Advanced Robotics). Springer Verlag, 2005.

[12] G. L. Beauregard and M. A. Srinivasan. The Manual Resolution of Viscosity and Mass. *ASME Dynamic Systems and Control Division*, 1:657–662, 1995.

[13] W. Becker, G. Nasios, S. Raab, and R. Jürgens. Fusion of Vestibular and Podokinesthetic Information During Self-turning Towards Instructed Targets. *Experimental Brain Research*, 144(4):458–74, 2002.

[14] M. Bergamasco, B. Allotta, L. Bosio, L. Ferretti, G. Perrini, G. M. Prisco, F. Salsedo, and G. Sartini. An Arm Exoskeleton System for Teleoperation and Virtual Environment Applications. In *Proceedings of the IEEE International Conference on Robotics and Automation*, pages 1449–1454, 1994.

[15] M. Bergamasco, A. Frisoli, and C. A. Avizzano. *Advances in Telerobotics*, chapter Exoskeletons as Man-Machine Interface Systems

for Teleoperation and Interaction in Virtual Environments , pages 61–76. STAR (Springer Tracts in Advanced Robotics). Springer Verlag, 2007.

[16] P. J. Berkelman, Z. J. Butler, and R. L. Hollis. Design of a Hemispherical Magnetic Levitation Haptic Interface Device. In *Proceedings of the ASME Winter Annual Meeting, Symposium on Haptic Interfaces for Virtual Environment and Teleoperator Systems*, pages 17–22, 1996.

[17] A. Bettini, S. Lang, A. Okamura, and G. Hager. Vision Assisted Control for Manipulation Using Virtual Fixtures. In *Proceedings of the IEEE/RSJ International Conference on Intelligent Robots and Systems*, pages 1171–1176, 2001.

[18] A. Bettini, S. Lang, A. Okamura, and G. Hager. Vision Assisted Control for Manipulation Using Virtual Fixtures: Experiments at Macro and Micro Scales. In *Proceedings of the IEEE International Conference on Robotics and Automation*, pages 3354–3361, 2002.

[19] A. Bettini, P. Marayong, S. Lang, A. M. Okamura, and G. D. Hager. Vision Assisted Control for Manipulation Using Virtual Fixtures. *IEEE Transactions on Robotics and Automation*, 20(6):953âĂŞ–966, 2004.

[20] F. Beutler and U. D. Hanebeck. Closed-Form Range-Based Posture Estimation Based on Decoupling Translation and Orientation. In *Proceedings of the 2005 IEEE International Conference on Acoustics, Speech, and Signal Processing (ICASSP 2005)*, volume 4, pages 989–992, Philadelphia, Pennsylvania, USA, Mar. 2005.

[21] H. Boessenkool, D. A. Abbink, and C. J. Heemskerk. Haptic Shared Control Improves Tele–Operated Task Performance towards Performance in Direct Control. In *Proceedings of the IEEE World Haptics Conference*, pages 433–438, 2011.

[22] D. Borro, J. Savall, A. Amundarain, J. J. Gil, A. García-Alonso, and L. Matey. A Large Haptic Device for Aircraft Engine Maintainability. *IEEE Computer Graphics and Applications*, 24(6):70–74, 2004.

[23] L. Bouguila, M. Ishii, and M. Sato. Multi-Modal Haptic Device for Large-Scale Virtual Environment. In *Proceedings of the 8th ACM Intl. Conference on Multimedia*, pages 277–283, 2000.

[24] E. S. Boy, E. Burdet, C. L. Teo, and J. E. Colgate. Investigation of Motion Guidance With Scooter Cobot and Collaborative Learning. *IEEE Transactions on Robotics*, 3(2):245–255, 2007.

[25] D. C. Brogan and N. L. Johnson. Realistic Human Walking Paths. In *Computer Animation and Social Agents (CASA)*, pages 94–101, 2003.

[26] G. Burdea. *Force and Touch Feedback for Virtual Reality*. John Wiley & Sons, 1996.

[27] C. Connolly, J. Burns, and R. Weiss. Path Planning Using Laplace's Equation. In *Proceedings of IEEE International Conference on Robotics and Automation*, 1990.

[28] R. Daily and D. M. Bevly. Harmonic Potential Field Path Planning for High Speed Vehicles. In *American Control Conference ACC*, 2008.

[29] R. P. Darken, T. Allard, and L. B. Achille. Spatial Orientation and Wayfinding in Large-Scale Virtual Spaces: An Introduction. *Presence*, 7(2):101–107, 1998.

[30] R. P. Darken, T. Allard, and L. B. Achille. Spatial Orientation and Wayfinding in Large-Scale Virtual Spaces ii. *Presence*, 8(6):iii–vi, 1999.

[31] S. Ekvall, D. Aarno, and D. Kragic. Online Task Recognition and Real–Time Adaptive Assistance for Computer-Aided Machine Control. *IEEE Transactions on Robotics*, 22:1029–1033, 2006.

[32] P. Evrard and A. Kheddar. Homotopy-Based Controller for Physical Human-Robot Interaction. In *Proceedings of the 18th IEEE International Symposium on Robot and Human Interactive Communication (RO-MAN)*, pages 1–6, 2009.

[33] D. Feygin, M. Keehner, and F. Tendick. Haptic Guidance: Experimental Evaluation of a Haptic Training Method for a Perceptual Motor Skill. In *Proceedings of the 10th Symp. On Haptic Interfaces For Virtual Envir. & Teleoperator Systs*, 2002.

[34] D. Flavigne, M. Taix, and E. Ferre. Interactive Motion Planning for Assembly Tasks. In *Proceedings of the 18th IEEE International Symposium onRobot and Human Interactive Communication (RO-MAN)*, pages 430–435, 2009.

[35] A. Formaglio, A. Giannitrapani, F. Barbagli, M. Franzini, and D. Prattichizzo. Performance of Mobile Haptic Interfaces. In *Proceedings of the 44th IEEE Conference on Decision and Control and the European Control Conference*, pages 8343–8348, 2005.

[36] B. A. Forsyth and K. E. MacLean. Predictive Haptic Guidance: Intelligent User Assistance for the Control of Dynamic Tasks. *IEEE Transactions on Visualization and Computer Graphics*, 12(1):103–113, 2006.

[37] M. Frey, D. E. Johnson, and J. Hollerbach. Full-Arm Haptics in an Accessibility Task. In *Proceedings of Symposium on Haptic Interfaces for Virtual Environment and Teleoperator Systems*, 2008.

[38] J. Funda, R. H. Taylor, B. Eldridge, S. Gomory, and K. G. Gruben. Constrained Cartesian Motion Control for Teleoperated Surgical Robots. *IEEE Transactions on Robotics and Automation*, 12(3):453âĂŞ–465, 1996.

[39] R. B. Gillespie, J. E. Colgate, and M. A. Peshkin. A General Framework for Cobot Control. *IEEE Transactions on Robotics and Automation*, 17(4):391–401, 2001.

[40] R. B. Gillespie, S. O'Modhrain, P. Tang, C. Pham, and D. Zaretsky. The Virtual Teacher. In *Proceedings of ASME International Mechanical Engineering Conference and Exposition*, 1998.

[41] M. Göller, F. Steinhardt, T. Kerscher, J. M. Zöllner, and R. Dillmann. Proactive Avoidance of Moving Obstacles for a Service Robot utilizing a Behavior-Based Control. In *Proceedings of IEEE/RSJ International Conference on Intelligent Robots and Systems*, pages 5984–5989, 2010.

[42] B. Graf. *Ein benutzer- und umgebungsangepasstes Steuerungssystem für die Zielführung roboterbasierter Gehhilfen*. PhD thesis, Universität Stuttgart, 2008.

[43] S. Grange, F. Conti, P. Rouiller, P. Helmer, and C. Baur. Overview of the Delta Haptic Device. In *Proceedings of the EuroHaptics Conference*, 2001.

[44] W. B. Griffin, W. R. Provancher, and M. R. Cutkosky. Feedback Strategies for Telemanipulation with Shared Control of Object Handling Forces. *Presence: Teleoperators and Virtual Environments*, 14(6):720–731, 2005.

[45] P. Griffiths and R. B. Gillespie. Sharing Control Between Human and Automation Using Haptic Interface: Primary and Secondary Task Performance Benefits. *Human Factors: The Journal of the Human Factors and Ergonomics Society*, 47(3):574–590, 2005.

[46] H. Gurocak, S. Jayaram, B. Parrish, and U. Jayaram. Weight Sensation in Virtual Environments Using a Haptic Device With Air Jets. *Journal of Computing and Information Science in Engineering*, 3(2):130–135, 2003.

[47] S. G. Hart and L. E. Stavenland. Development of NASA-TLX (Task Load Index): Results of Empirical and Theoretical Research. In P. A. Hancock and N. Meshkati, editors, *Human Mental Workload*, chapter 7, pages 139–183. Elsevier, 1988.

[48] K. Hashtrudi-Zaad and S. E. Salcudean. Analysis of Control Architectures for Teleoperation Systems with Impedance/Admittance Master and Slave Manipulators. *The International Journal of Robotics Research*, 20(6):419–445, 2001.

[49] V. Hayward. Is There a âĂŸPlenhapticâĂŹ Function? *Philosophical Transactions of the Royal Society B: Biological Sciences*, 366(1581):3115–3122, 2011.

[50] V. Hayward and O. R. Astley. Performance Measures for Haptic Interfaces. In *Proceedings of the 7th International Symposium in Robotics Research*, pages 195–207, 1996.

[51] C. Herrmann and F. Romahn. Evaluierung und Vergleich des neuen haptischen Manipulators für das Holodeck. Research Project Report, Intelligent Sensor-Actuator-Systems Laboratory, Karlsruher Institut für Technologie (KIT), unpublished, February 2011.

[52] J. Hollerbach, D. Grow, and C. Parker. Developments in Locomotion Interfaces. In *Proceedings of 9th International Conference on Rehabilitation Robotics*, pages 522–525, 2005.

[53] J. M. Hollerbach. Some Current Issues in Haptics Research. In *Proceedings of the IEEE Intl. Conference on Robotics and Automation*, pages 757–762, 2000.

[54] T. Huang, M. Li, Z. Li, D. Chetwynd, and D. Whitehouse. Optimal Kinematic Design of 2-DOF Parallel Manipulators with Well-Shaped Workspace Bounded by a Specified Conditioning Index. *IEEE Transactions on Robotics and Automation*, 20(3):538–543, 2004.

[55] J. Huegel and M. O'Malley. Progressive Haptic and Visual Guidance for Training in a Virtual Dynamic Task. In *Proceedings of the IEEE Haptics Symposium*, pages 343–350, 2010.

[56] H. Iwata. The Torus Treadmill: Realizing Locomotion in VEs. *IEEE Computer Graphics and Applications*, 19(6):30–35, 1999.

[57] H. Iwata, H. Yano, H. Fukushima, and H. Noma. CirculaFloor. *IEEE Computer Graphics and Applications*, 25(1):64–67, 2005.

[58] H. Iwata, H. Yano, and F. Nakaizumi. Gait Master: A Versatile Locomotion Interface for Uneven Virtual Terrain. In *Proceedings of the IEEE Virtual Reality Conference*, pages 131–137, 2001.

[59] L. D. Joly and C. Andriot. Imposing Motion Constraints to a Force Reflecting Telerobot through Real-Time Simulation of a Virtual Mechanism. In *Proceedings of the IEEE International Conference on Robotics and Automation*, pages 357–362, 1995.

[60] L. A. Jones and I. W. Hunter. Human Operator Perception of Mechanical Variables and their Effects on Tracking Performance. *Advances in Robotics*, 42:49–53, 1992.

[61] A. Kapoor, M. Li, and R. H. Taylor. Constrained Control for Surgical Assistant Robots. In *Proceedings of the IEEE International Conference on Robotics and Automation*, pages 231–236, 2006.

[62] S. Karlin. Raiding Iron Man's Closet [Geek Life]. *IEEE Spectrum*, 48(8):25–25, 2011.

[63] O. Khatib. Real-Time Obstacle Avoidance for Manipulators and Mobile Robots. *International Journal of Robotics Research*, 5(1):90–98, 1986.

[64] A. Kheddar, C. Tzafestas, and P. Coiffet. The Hidden Robot Concept – High Level Abstraction Teleoperation. In *Proceedings of the IEEE/RSJ International Conference on Intelligent Robots and Systems*, 1997.

[65] R. Kikuuwe and T. Yoshikawa. Haptic Display Device with Fingertip Presser for Motion/Force Teaching to Human. In *Proceedings of the IEEE International Conference on Robotics and Automation*, pages 868–873, 2001.

[66] J. Kim, P. H. Chang, and H.-S. Park. Transparent Teleoperation Using Two-Channel Control Architectures. In *Proceedings of IEEE/RSJ International Conference on Intelligent Robots and Systems*, pages 1953–1960, 2005.

[67] J. O. Kim and P. Khosla. Real-Time Obstacle Avoidance Using Harmonic Potential Functions. *IEEE Transactions on Robotics and Automation*, 8(3):338–349, 1992.

[68] E. P. Klement, R. Mesiar, and E. Pap. *Triangular Norms (Trends in Logic)* . Springer-Verlag, 2000.

[69] N. Klopčar and J. Lenarčič. Kinematic Model for Determination of Human Arm Reachable Workspace. *Meccanica*, 40:203–219, 2005.

[70] D. Kragić, P. Marayong, M. Li, A. M. Okamura, and G. D. Hager. Human-Machine Collaborative Systems for Microsurgical Applications. *The International Journal of Robotics Research*, 24(9):731–741, 2005.

[71] T. Kretz, A. Große, S. Hengst, L. Kautzsch, A. Pohlmann, and P. Vortisch. Quickest Paths in Simulations of Pedestrians. *Advances in Complex Systems*, pages 733–759, 2011.

[72] U. Künzler and C. Runde. Kinesthetic Haptics Integration into Large-Scale Virtual Environments. In *Proceedings of the First Joint Eurohaptics Conference and Symposium on Haptic Interfaces for Virtual Environment and Teleoperator Systems. World Haptics Conference*, pages 551–556, 2005.

[73] D. A. Lawrence. Stability and Transparency in Bilateral Teleoperation. *IEEE Transactions on Robotics and Automation*, 9(5):624–637, 1993.

[74] D. A. Lawrence and J. D. Chapel. Performance Trade-Offs for Hand Controller Design. In *Proceedings of IEEE International Conference on Robotics and Automation*, pages 3211–3216, 1994.

[75] M. Li, M. Ishii, and R. H. Taylor. Spatial Motion Constraints Using Virtual Fixtures Generated by Anatomy. *IEEE Transactions on Robotics*, 23(1):4–29, 2007.

[76] M. Li and A. M. Okamura. Recognition of Operator Motions for Real-Time Assistance using Virtual Fixtures. In *Proceedings of 11th Symposium on Haptic Interfaces for Virtual Environments and Teleoperator Systems*, pages 125–131, 2003.

[77] P. Marayong, M. Li, A. M. Okamura, and G. D. Hager. Spatial Motion Constraints: Theory and Demonstrations for Robot Guidance

Using Virtual Fixtures. In *Proceedings of IEEE International Conference on Robotics and Automation*, 2003.

[78] P. Marayong and A. Okamura. Speed-Accuracy Characteristics of Human-Machine Cooperative Manipulation using Virtual Fixtures with Variable Admittance . *Human Factors: The Journal of the Human Factors and Ergonomics Society*, 46(3):518–532, 2004.

[79] J. Martin and J. Savall. Mechanisms for Haptic Torque Feedback. In *Proceedings of the First Joint Eurohaptics Conference and Symposium on Haptic Interfaces for Virtual Environments and Teleoperator Systems*, 2005.

[80] T. Massie and J. Salisbury. The PHANTOM Haptic Interface: A Device for Probing Virtual Objects. In *Proceedings of the ASME Winter Annual Meeting: Dynamic Systems and Control Division*, volume 55, pages 295–301, 1994.

[81] N. Nitzsche. *Weiträumige Telepräsenz: Unbeschränkte Fortbewegung und haptische Interaktion*. Number 1095 in Fortschritt-Berichte Reihe: Mess-, Steuerungs- und Regelungstechnik. VDI Verlag, Düsseldorf, 2006.

[82] N. Nitzsche, U. D. Hanebeck, and G. Schmidt. Design Issues of Mobile haptic Interfaces. *Journal of Robotic Systems*, 20:9:549–556, 2003.

[83] N. Nitzsche, U. D. Hanebeck, and G. Schmidt. Motion Compression for Telepresent Walking in Large Target Environments. *Presence*, 13(1):44–60, 2004.

[84] N. Nitzsche and G. Schmidt. A Mobile Haptic Interface Mastering a Mobile Teleoperator. In *Proceedings of IEEE/RSJ International Conference on Intelligent Robots and Systems*, 2004.

[85] M. K. O'Malley and A. Gupta. Passive and Active Assistance for Human Performance of a Simulated Underactuated Dynamic Task. In *Proceedings of the 11th Symposium on Haptic Interfaces for Virtual Environments and Teleoperator Systems*, 2003.

[86] S. Park, R. Howe, and D. Torchiana. Virtual Fixtures for Robotic Cardiac Surgery. In *Proceedings of International Conference on Medical Image Computing and Computer Assisted Intervention*, pages 1419–1420, 2001.

[87] C. Passenberg, R. Groten, A. Peer, and M. Buss. Towards Real–Time Haptic Assistance Adaptation Optimizing Task Performance and Human Effort. In *Proceedings of the IEEE World Haptics Conference*, pages 155–160, 2011.

[88] C. Passenberg, V. Nitsch, U. Unterhinninghofen, B. Färber, and M. Buss. Position and Force Augmentation in a Telepresence System and Their Effects on Perceived Realism. In *Proceedings of the Third Joint Eurohaptics Conference and Symposium on Haptic Interfaces for Virtual Environments and Teleoperator Systems*, 2009.

[89] C. Passenberg, A. Peer, and M. Buss. A Survey of Environment-, Operator-, and Task-Adapted Controllers for Teleoperation Systems. *Journal of Mechatronics (Spec. Iss. on Design & Control Methodologies in Telerobotics)*, 20(7):787–801, 2010.

[90] S. Payandeh and Z. Stanisic. On Application of Virtual Fixtures as an Aid for Telemanipulation and Training. In *Proceedings of Symposium on Haptic Interfaces for Virtual Environments and Teleoperator Systems*, pages 18–23, 2002.

[91] A. Peer. *Design and Control of Admittance-Type Telemanipulation Systems*. Number 1154 in Fortschritt-Berichte Reihe: Mess-, Steuerungs- und Regelungstechnik. VDI Verlag, Düsseldorf, 2008.

[92] A. Peer, Y.Komoguchi, and M. Buss. Towards a Mobile Haptic Interface for Bimanual Manipulations. In *Proceedings of the IEEE/RSJ International Conference on Intelligent Robots and Systems*, pages 384–391, 2007.

[93] J. Perry and J. Rosen. Design of a 7 Degree-of-Freedom Upper-Limb Powered Exoskeleton. In *The First IEEE/RAS-EMBS International Conference on Biomedical Robotics and Biomechatronics (BioRob 2006)*, pages 805–810, 2006.

[94] M. A. Peshkin, J. E. Colgate, W. Wannasuphoprasit, C. A. Moore, R. B. Gillespie, and P. Akella. Cobot Architecture. *IEEE Transactions Robotics and Automation*, 17(4):377–390, 2001.

[95] B. Peterson, M. Wells, T. A. Furness III, and E. Hunt. The Effects of the Interface on Navigation in Virtual Environments. In *Proceedings of Human Factors and Ergonomics Society 1998 Annual Meeting*, pages 1496–1505, 1998.

[96] Z. Pezzementi, A. M. Okamura, and G. D. Hager. Dynamic Guidance with Pseudoadmittance Virtual Fixtures. In *Proceedings of the International Conference on Robotics and Automation*, 2007.

[97] H. Pongrac, B. Färber, P. Hinterseer, J. Kammerl, and E. Steinbach. Limitations of Human 3D Force Discrimination. In *Human-Centered Robotics Systems*, 2006.

[98] D. Powell and M. K. O'Malley. Efficacy of Shared-Control Guidance Paradigms for Robot-Mediated Training. In *Proceedings of IEEE World Haptics Conference*, pages 427–432, 2011.

[99] J. Ren, R. V. Patel, K. A. McIsaac, G. Guiraudon, and T. M. Peters. Dynamic 3-D Virtual Fixtures for Minimally Invasive Beating Heart Procedures. *IEEE Transactions on Medical Imaging*, 27(8):1061–1070, 2008.

[100] C. Richard and M. R. Cutkosky. Contact Force Perception with an Ungrounded Haptic Interface. In *Proceedingsof ASME IMECE 6th Annual Symposium on Haptic Interfaces*, 1997.

[101] B. E. Riecke. *How Far Can We Get with Just Visual Information? Path Integration and Spatial Updating Studies in Virtual Reality.* PhD thesis, Eberhard-Karls-Universität zu Tübingen, 2003.

[102] E. Rimon and D. E. Koditschek. The Construction of Analytic Diffeomorphismus for Exact Robot Navigation on Star Worlds. In *Proceedings of IEEE International Conference on Robotics and Automation*, pages 21–26, 1989.

[103] J. Rosell and P. Iñiguez. Path Planning using Harmonic Functions and Probabilistic Cell Decomposition. In *Proceedings of the 2005 IEEE International Conference on Robotics and Automation*, pages 1803–1808, 2005.

[104] J. Rosell, C. Vázquez, A. Pérez, and P. Iñiguez. Motion Planning for Haptic Guidance. *Journal of Intelligent and Robotic Systems*, 53:223–245, 2008.

[105] L. Rosenberg. Virtual Fixtures: Perceptual Tools for Telerobotic Manipulation. In *Proceedings of IEEE Virtual Reality International Symposium*, pages 76–82, 1993.

[106] P. Rößler. *Telepräsente Bewegung und haptische Interaktion in ausgedehnten entfernten Umgebungen.* Number 3 in Karlsruhe Series on Intelligent Sensor-Actuator-Systems, Universität Karlsruhe / Intelligent Sensor-Actuator-Systems Laboratory. KIT Scientific Publishing, Karlsruhe, 2009.

[107] P. Rößler, T. Armstrong, O. Hessel, M. Mende, and U. D. Hanebeck. A Novel Haptic Interface for Free Locomotion in Extended Range

Telepresence Scenarios. In *Proceedings of the 3rd International Conference on Informatics in Control, Automation and Robotics (ICINCO 2006)*, pages 148–153, Setubal, Portugal, 2006.

[108] P. Rößler and U. D. Hanebeck. Simultaneous Motion Compression for Multi-User Extended Range Telepresence. In *Proceedings of the IEEE/RSJ International Conference on Intelligent Robots and Systems (IROS'06)*, Beijing, China, 2006.

[109] P. Rößler, U. D. Hanebeck, and N. Nitzsche. Feedback Controlled Motion Compression for Extended Range Telepresence. In *Proceedings of IEEE Mechatronics & Robotics (MechRob'04), Special Session on Telepresence and Teleaction*, pages 1447–1452, Aachen, Germany, 2004.

[110] P. Rößler, O. C. Schrempf, and U. D. Hanebeck. Stochastic Prediction of Waypoints for Extended Range Telepresence Applications. In *Proceedings of Second International Workshop on Human Centered Robotic Systems (HCRS'06)*, Munich, Germany, 2006.

[111] A. Schiele and G. Visentin. The ESA Human Arm Exoskeleton for Space Robotics. In *Proceedings of the 7th International Symposium on Artificial Intelligence, Robotics and Automation in Space*, 2003.

[112] T. B. Sheridan. Telerobotics. *Automatica*, 25(4):487–507, 1989.

[113] T. B. Sheridan. Telerobotics, Automation, and Human Supervisory Control. MIT Press, 1992.

[114] B. Siciliano, L. Sciavicco, L. Villani, and G. Oriolo. *Robotics: Modelling, Planning and Control*. Advanced Textbooks in Control and Signal Processing. Springer-Verlag, 2010.

[115] H. J. Sussmann. A General Theorem of Symmetries and Local Controllability. In *Proc. of the 24th IEEE Conference on Decision and Control*, volume 24, pages 27–32, 1985.

[116] H. Z. Tan, F. Barbagli, K. Salisbury, C. Ho, and C. Spence. Force-Direction Discrimination is not Influenced by Reference Force Direction. *Haptics-e*, 4:1–6, 2006.

[117] M. J. Tarr and W. H. Warren. Virtual Reality in Behavioral Neuroscience and Beyond. *Nature Neuroscience Supplement*, 5:1089–1092, 2002.

[118] M. O. Tokhi and A. K. M. Azad, editors. *Flexible Robot Manipulators: Modelling, Simulation, and Control*, volume 68 of *Control Engineering Series*. Institution of Engineering and Technology, London, 2008.

[119] N. Tsagarakis, D. G. Caldwell, and G. A. Medrano-Cerda. A 7 DOF Pneumatic Muscle Actuator (pMA) Powered Exoskeleton. In *Proceedings of the 8th IEEE International Workshop in Robot and Human Interaction*, pages 327–333, 1999.

[120] N. Turro, O. Khatib, and E. Coste-Maniere. Haptically Augmented Teleoperation. In *Proceedings of the 2001 IEEE International Conference on Robotics & Automation*, 2001.

[121] M. W. Ueberle. *Design, Control, and Evaluation of a Family of Kinesthetic Haptic Interfaces*. Number 1113 in Fortschritt-Berichte Reihe: Mess-, Steuerungs- und Regelungstechnik. VDI, Dachau, 2006.

[122] M. W. Ueberle and M. Buss. Control of Kinesthetic Haptic Interfaces. In *Proceedings of the IEEE/RSJ International Conference on Intelligent Robots and Systems. Workshop on Touch and Haptics*, 2004.

[123] M. W. Ueberle, N. Mock, and M. Buss. VISHARD10, A Novel Hyper–Redundant Haptic Interface. In *Proceedings of the 12th International Symposium on Haptic Interfaces for Virtual Environments and Teleoperator Systems*, pages 58–65, 2004.

[124] U. Unterhinninghofen, F. K. B. Freyberger, and M. Buss. Study on Computer Assistance for Telepresent Reaching Movements. In *Proceedings of the 6th International Conference on Haptics: Perception, Devices and Scenarios*, 2008.

[125] R. Q. van der Linde, P. Lammertse, E. Frederiksen, and B. Ruiter. The HapticMaster, a New High-Performance Haptic Interface. In *Proceedings of the EuroHaptics Conference*, pages 1–5, 2002.

[126] R. Volpe. *Teleoperation and Robotics in Space*, chapter Techniques for Collision Prevention, Impact Stability, and Force Control by Space Manipulators, pages 175–208. AIAA, 1994.

[127] H. Yano, M. Yoshie, and H. Iwata. Development of a Non-Grounded Haptic Interface Using the Gyro Effect. In *Proceeding of the 11th Symposium on Haptic Interfaces for Virtual Environment and Teleoperator Systems*, pages 32–39, 2003.

[128] J. Yoon, J. Park, and J. Ryu. Walking Control of a Dual-Planar Parallel Robot for Omni-Directional Locomotion Interface. In *Proceedings of IEEE/RSJ International Conference on Intelligent Robots and Systems*, pages 1151 – 1156, 2005.

[129] T. Yoshikawa. Manipulability and Redundancy Control of Robotic Mechanisms. In *Proceedings of IEEE International Conference on Robotics and Automation*, pages 1004–1009, 1985.

[130] F. Zacharias, I. Howard, T. Hulin, and G. Hirzinger. Workspace Comparisons of Setup Configurations for Human-Robot Interaction.

In *Proceedings of IEEE/RSJ International Conference on Intelligent Robots and Systems*, pages 3117–3122, 2010.

[131] M. H. Zadeh, D. Wang, and E. Kubica. *Advances in Haptics*, chapter Factors Affecting the Perception-Based Compression of Haptic Data, pages 517–542. InTech, 2010.

[132] J. S. Zelek and M. D. Levine. Local-Global Concurrent Path Planning and Execution. *IEEE Transactions on Systems, Man and Cybernetics, Part A: Systems and Humans*, 30(6):865–870, 2000.

Supervised Student Theses

[133] S. Bumm. Entwurf eines leichten Manipulators für weiträumige haptische Interaktion (Design of a Light Manipulator for Extended Range Haptic Interaction). Student research project, Intelligent Sensor-Actuator-Systems Laboratory, Karlsruher Institut für Technologie (KIT), 2010.

[134] T. Hanke. Weiträumige haptische Benutzerführung mittels einer hochauflösenden Plenhaptic Guidance Function (Wide–Area Haptic Guidance using a High–Resolution Plenhaptic Guidance Function). Bachelor thesis, Intelligent Sensor-Actuator-Systems Laboratory, Karlsruher Institut für Technologie (KIT), 2011.

[135] F. Packi. Darstellung definierter Kräfte aus einer Telepräsenzumgebung auf einer großen haptischen Schnittstelle (Display of Defined Forces from the Target Environment on a Large Haptic Display). Student research project, Intelligent Sensor-Actuator-Systems Laboratory, Universität Karlsruhe (TH), 2007.

[136] F. Packi. Entwurf und Implementierung eines eingebetteten drahtlosen akustischen Trackingsystems (Design and Implementation of an Embedded Wireless Acoustic Trackingsystem). Diploma thesis, Intelligent Sensor-Actuator-Systems Laboratory, Universität Karlsruhe (TH), 2009.

[137] F. Pfaff. Kontextbasierte haptische Benutzerführung in einem weiträumigen Szenario (Context–based Haptic Guidance in an Extended Range Scenario). Student research project, Intelligent

Sensor-Actuator-Systems Laboratory, Karlsruher Institut für Technologie (KIT), 2011.

[138] O. Richter. Regelung einer großen haptischen Schnittstelle (Control of a Large Haptic Interface). Diploma thesis, Intelligent Sensor-Actuator-Systems Laboratory, Universität Karlsruhe (TH), 2008.

[139] A. Runte. Generierung von Stereo–Ansichten einer realen Umgebung auf Basis einer Bilddatenbank (Generation of Stereo–views from a Real Environment by means of an Image–database). Student research project, Intelligent Sensor-Actuator-Systems Laboratory, Karlsruher Institut für Technologie (KIT), 2010.

Own Publications

[140] T. Kretz, S. Hengst, A. Pérez Arias, S. Friedberger, and U. D. Hanebeck. Using Extended Range Telepresence to Investigate Route Choice Behavior. In *Proceedings of the Traffic and Granular Flow Conference 2011 (TGF 2011)*, Moscow, Russia, Sept. 2011.

[141] T. Kretz, S. Hengst, V. Roca, A. Pérez Arias, S. Friedberger, and U. D. Hanebeck. Calibrating Dynamic Pedestrian Route Choice with an Extended Range Telepresence System. In *Proceedings of the first IEEE Workshop on Modeling, Simulation and Visual Analysis of Large Crowds in conjunction with the 13th International Conference on Computer Vision (ICCV 2011)*, Barcelona, Spain, Nov. 2011.

[142] T. Kretz, A. Pérez Arias, S. Friedberger, and U. D. Hanebeck. Using Extended Range Telepresence to Collect Data of Pedestrian Dynamics. In *Proceedings of the Transportation Research Board's 91st Annual Meeting (TRB 2012)* , Washington D.C., Jan. 2012.

[143] F. Packi, A. Pérez Arias, F. Beutler, and U. D. Hanebeck. A Wearable System for the Wireless Experience of Extended Range Telepresence. In *Proceedings of the 2010 IEEE/RSJ International Conference on Intelligent Robots and Systems (IROS 2010)*, Taipei, Taiwan, Oct. 2010.

[144] A. Pérez Arias, H. P. Eberhardt, F. Pfaff, and U. D. Hanebeck. The Plenhaptic Guidance Function for Intuitive Navigation in Extended Range Telepresence Scenarios. In *Proceedings of the IEEE World Haptics Conference (WHC 2011)*, Istanbul, Turkey, June 2011.

[145] A. Pérez Arias and U. D. Hanebeck. A Novel Haptic Interface for Extended Range Telepresence: Control and Evaluation. In *Proceedings of the 6th International Conference on Informatics in Control, Automation and Robotics (ICINCO 2009)*, pages 222–227, Milan, Italy, July 2009.

[146] A. Pérez Arias and U. D. Hanebeck. Wide-Area Haptic Guidance: Taking the User by the Hand. In *Proceedings of the 2010 IEEE/RSJ International Conference on Intelligent Robots and Systems (IROS 2010)*, Taipei, Taiwan, Oct. 2010.

[147] A. Pérez Arias and U. D. Hanebeck. Motion Control of a Semi-Mobile Haptic Interface for Extended Range Telepresence. In *Proceedings of the 2011 IEEE/RSJ International Conference on Intelligent Robots and Systems (IROS 2011)*, San Francisco, California, Sept. 2011.

[148] A. Pérez Arias, T. Kretz, P. Ehrhardt, S. Hengst, P. Vortisch, and U. D. Hanebeck. A Framework for Evaluating the VISSIM Traffic Simulation with Extended Range Telepresence. In *Proceedings of the 22nd Annual Conference on Computer Animation and Social Agents (CASA 2009)*, pages 13–16, Amsterdam, The Netherlands, June 2009.

[149] A. Pérez Arias, T. Kretz, P. Ehrhardt, S. Hengst, P. Vortisch, and U. D. Hanebeck. Extended Range Telepresence for Evacuation Training in Pedestrian Simulations. In *Proceedings of the 5th International Conference on Pedestrian and Evacuation Dynamics (PED 2010), Springer-Verlag*, Gaithersburg, Maryland, Mar. 2010.

Karlsruhe Series on Intelligent Sensor-Actuator-Systems

Edited by Prof. Dr.-Ing. Uwe D. Hanebeck // ISSN 1867-3813

Die Bände sind unter www.ksp.kit.edu als PDF frei verfügbar oder als Druckausgabe bestellbar.

Karlsruhe Series on Intelligent Sensor-Actuator-Systems

Edited by Prof. Dr.-Ing. Uwe D. Hanebeck // ISSN 1867-3813

Die Bände sind unter www.ksp.kit.edu als PDF frei verfügbar oder als Druckausgabe bestellbar.